To Patricia & Stan,
Best Wishes!

Rick
Jurmanek
10/11/97

Good Luck w/Your Book!!

D0021128

In Memory of
Paul Edward Tatum
Entrepreneur, Visionary and Economic Genius

For every copy of *Stranded in Moscow*
you purchase, Square Peg Press
will make a donation to the
Paul Tatum Memorial Fund

For further information, you may write
Square Peg Press™
PO Box 2194
Gilbert, Arizona 85299

Library of Congress Catalog Card Number   96-71741

ISBN   0-9655703-5-5

Printed in the United States of America

01   00   99   98   97 / 5   4   3   2   1

STRANDED

IN

MOSCOW

AN AMERICAN'S STORY OF LIFE IN THE NEW RUSSIA

RICK FURMANEK

For my wife, Robin Elizabeth,
the undying romance in my life

For my son, Seth Edward,
the ever-present passion in my life

For my daughter, Lindsay Elizabeth,
the never-ending joy in my life

I thank you
for persevering courageously,
while laughing wholeheartedly,
and loving unconditionally

Without each of you,
I would have no story to tell

CONTENTS

ACKNOWLEDGMENTS

I wish to express my sincere gratitude for the friends and family who touched our lives while preparing for our move to Moscow. Mark and Tam for helping pave the way. The CDO family for a place to lick our wounds. The guys in the band. Troy and Lisa for the pizza. Tim and Pam for sending us off with style. Morris and Barbara for opening up your home to us.

For those who upheld us while in Moscow, our lives wouldn't be the same without each of you. Louis, Shelley and Amy for your constant lifeline back to the States. Trish and Steve for holding down the fort. Ed and Millie for your never-ceasing encouragement. The International Christian Assembly family for a place to hang out hat. Bopper for your positive words in the midst of your own heartache. New Life Christian School for allowing an exception. The architects, project managers and support staff in Moscow, Dave, Clive, Garrick, Bill, Eric, Peter, Jim, Oxana, Svetlana, Julia and Sergei. Mike C. for words of comfort that fateful night. Taliessa for sending us a little bit of home. Claudio, you're a true gentleman.

To those who encouraged the forthcoming of this book since our return to the States, you will not be forgotten. Kathy S. for proof-reading the technical side. Stan E. for your helpful suggestions. Julian and Justin for your constant support while I labored. Jeff G. for the software and masterful consultation. Kevin H. for your belief in my project. David B. for urging me into new frontiers. Buzz for your kind words. Kristen S. for the Macintosh® goodies. Carolyn H. and Mike F. for your excitement. Jeff B. for your never-ceasing prayer. Jessica P. for becoming my first fan. Steve T. for your connections. Ron, for your discerning eye and positive suggestions about the cover design. Chris, Augie, Paul, James, Eric, Laura, Marc, Carolyn, Chris, Victoria and Glenda for your positive doses of enthusiasm. Rick O. for your life of consistency. David, my long lost brother, literally, for adding a new dimension in my life. Mom for your love of reading and your insistence on adding this book to your own "best seller" list. John Dorminy, for your kindness and generous spirit. You helped make it happen.

We could not forget our Russian soulmates, Andrei, Lydia, Alla, Katia, Anton, Lena, Yelena, Olga, Olga, Olga and Olga, Sasha, Natasha, Uri, Oleg and Valentina, and Misha. Thank you for captivating our hearts and unlocking the mystery of Russia.

Finally, for Paul Tatum, American executive and beloved brother tragically murdered, gunned down by the Russian mafia on the streets of Moscow. They may have silenced your voice, but your spirit lives on.

1
MOSCOW
MIRACLES
AND MOSES

Staring out the tiny window at the thick mass of snow clouds swarming below us, I began to retrace each step of my family's last two weeks in the States. If given the opportunity, I don't think I could have staged a more bizarre departure than the one we experienced. The delay of our scheduled departure for Russia had forced us to scramble for some temporary living arrangements. In desperation for a place to stay, we found ourselves driving up to a diminutive one bedroom mobile home that sat in the middle of a semi-trailer's graveyard. Once filled with hazardous waste, including radiation refuse, the twisted pieces of metal were vivid reminders of the dangers of sleeping while driving.

Temporarily vacant, in between trucker's stints, the dwelling offered no pretense of being a home, or anything else that we had ever encountered. We found ourselves surrounded with radiation danger signs everywhere we looked.

The hazardous living conditions weren't the only concern, a corroded shower faucet, only giving up a drizzle of rusty, lead-filled water, a rocking toilet on particleboard so waterlogged that you feared the next time you sat down you might go through, a kitchen counter so warped dishes would slide one way or the other depending on how the food was arranged on the plate, and a waterbed, intended for two, that only slept one comfortably were daily obstacles to overcome. Emergency phone calls in the middle of the night, loud sirens and horns set to go off at any time, and strangers walking in unannounced, expecting to use the restroom, were a part of our daily routine as well. *Was this a sign of things to come,* I wondered.

"We apologize, ladies and gentlemen," the flight attendant interrupted my thoughts, attempting to communicate with the few English speaking passengers on board through her thick Slavic accent. "*Sheremetyevo II* has been experiencing some difficulties with the snow storm. They have just reopened the airport and have cleared us for landing. I am sorry to say that the automatic ramp for disembarking is frozen and inoperable, so as we begin to land we must inform you that we will be disembarking outside."

"Welcome to Moscow," I muttered.

"Ladies and gentlemen," the flight attendant interrupted once again. "The Captain has informed me that the temperature at *Sheremetyevo II* is minus ten degrees

Celsius with high winds and blowing snow. As you disembark, there will be *Militsiya* to guide you. Please be very careful. There is much snow and ice."

Robin and I looked at each other in disbelief. "The kid's heavy coats are in the luggage, not in our carry-ons," she said. "I didn't want to load us down too much. Honey, what are we going to do? The kids will freeze." Robin's tone of voice carried her discouragement, her sense of helplessness and frustration. These feelings, we would soon find out, were ones that we would become acquainted with on a daily basis.

Keeping warm was only one of the elements to deal with. Walking down a flight of ice-laden steel stairs toting eight oversized carry-ons and two small children, and not knowing who or how to ask for help, was definitely the greater obstacle.

The jet descended through the gray clouds, full of both snow and pollution. Once beneath these clouds, the land stretched out and revealed something I hadn't expected. I saw trees, lots of trees. Evergreens and birch trees were everywhere. They seemed to engulf plot after plot of white frozen farmland.

And there were gray apartment buildings, known in Russia as flats. The skyline seemed littered with them as far as the eye could see. Some were tall, fifteen stories or more, some were smaller, three to four stories high. The horizon was also flat, there were no mountains, just a few rolling hills.

We glided over the runway and heard the familiar

screech of the wheels touching down.   Landing in
Moscow stirred up a storm of emotions within me. It
seems that just the mention of Moscow stirred up the
same flurry of mixed emotions in people we encountered while preparing to embark on our journey. Their
responses became all the more intense when we
informed them that we were getting ready to move to
Moscow.   One of two reactions were typical: "That
sounds fascinating. I wish I were doing that. What an
opportunity." or "Why in the world would you want to
go there? Are you taking your children with you?" The
long American tradition of distrust and prejudice
toward Russia became increasingly evident as we found
ourselves having to defend our move more and more
often.

I was told that the *Sheremetyevo II* airport had been
built for the 1980 Olympics to accommodate international flights. It, too, was gray. The airport seemed starved
for attention, appearing to have received little since 1980.
I immediately sensed a crumbling infrastructure, a desperate society, and landing at dusk added to the gray-
ness of it all.

After taxing around the airport for what seemed to be
an abnormally long time, we finally found our spot next
to the frozen ramp. We had already decided from our
most recent experience, that we would be the last family
off the jet. No sense in fighting it. Two kids and eight

carry-ons tended to make others impatient. It also gave us the time we needed to come up with some creative ways to bundle the kids.

The arctic blast blew through the interior of the fuselage. Robin had decided to wrap Lindsay, our youngest, with her own coat. I wrapped Seth in my light windbreaker, layering it over his jean jacket. I thought the carry-ons would provide somewhat of a windbreak for myself and Robin. Stepping out onto the icy stairs immediately erased that idea.

Standing at the bottom of the stairs prepared to guide the passengers was a stoic-looking soldier. He offered no smile, no hand, no help. It wasn't his job. His job was to make sure that everyone was headed, or herded, in the right direction. The gun hanging off his shoulder ensured that. The soldier's cold, suspicious stare was enhanced by the cloud of steam spewing from his nose.

The frigid air froze the hair in my nostrils. I could only imagine what it was doing to the kids. We made our move down the stairs. The flight attendant attempted to assist us as much as possible. I'm sure we looked quite out of place, underdressed Americans in a Moscow blizzard.

I can honestly say to this day that I have no idea how we made it to the terminal, but we all gasped a sigh of relief when the warmer air of the building hit us.

With barely a moment to catch our breath and collect our bearings, we were immediately shoved forward, almost against our will, by a new group behind us who had just arrived on another flight. They were pushing us into a seemingly endless sea of people moving toward the narrow bottleneck of the first inspection point. Passengers were being released one at a time into the passport/visa area. We felt like well-chilled molasses moving through a tiny hour glass. On both sides of the passageway were huge glass windows with military officials standing behind them inspecting the crowd like cattlemen attending an auction.

"Mommy, I got to go potty," Lindsay said.

"It'll be okay," Robin said. "We'll be finished in just a moment."

We glanced at each other, knowing the wait would be much longer. As is typical of a two-year-old while in potty training, Lindsay's urgency and frustration mounted with each passing moment. She squealed and stomped her feet while grabbing at her crotch.

Somewhere in the crowd right before us we heard a booming Russian voice utter something that sounded like a command. It startled us, but the result of the command was even more dramatic. Like Moses at the Red Sea, the entire crowd parted right before us and we were quickly ushered to the front of the group.

That day we witnessed first hand a wonderful custom. If you have young children, you automatically get to go to the front of the line, without discussion. That's one benefit of being the parent of a small child in a crowded Russian airport.

"Proceed to the passport/visa inspection gate, sir,"

said a young pimply-faced soldier as he motioned us toward one of the vacant windows, each with its own gate that opened into the baggage claim area.

We towed our belongings up to a window and immediately noticed the oversized mirror above us, set at an angle where the inspection officer could see exactly what we carried in our hands.

"Lindsay, come back here," Robin shouted.

The young soldier had not yet cleared us but Lindsay refused to wait. She climbed through the gate and quickly scampered off toward the baggage claim area. Behind the window, the young soldier's face quickly soured. With the flailing of his hands, he demanded that Robin and I corner Lindsay, and bring her back. His body language was easy enough to understand without him having to say a word.

Once we retrieved Lindsay, he resumed his duty. "Why is name Duncan on passport and Furmanek on visa?" the stern-faced young soldier demanded.

"Ah, we have just had our last name changed," I replied. "Please look in the back of the passport and you will see the notification." He examined the back of the passport. He examined the front of the passport. Then he examined the passport some more. He stood up and quickly exited the booth.

Oh great, I thought, *they're going to interrogate my family, probably do a strip search, put us under a spotlight for questioning, confiscate our luggage.*

The young soldier returned just as quickly with an

apparent supervisor. He was older and had more medals on his uniform than the younger man questioning us. They uttered a few sentences back and forth in Russian and seemed very engrossed in our documents.

The supervisor turned to me, took a slow drag on his cigarette while thumbing through my passport, and said, "Why did you change your name?"

I leaned down and attempted to speak as clearly as possible through the small slot in the glass window. I spoke loudly and slowly, as if that would help him understand English.

"You see, I have decided to take my real father's name. We did this just before we left,"

I was ready to go into great detail on how I had discovered my real father's name and how we had gone to court in order to get it changed, when he reached for his stamp and pounded our passports and visas repeatedly. He then attempted to instruct me in sign language not to fold the visas the way I had. Although it seemed logical to fold them to fit neatly into the protective covering of the Passport, we soon discovered that logic had little meaning in the stubborn ways of the Russian people.

U nas poryadok takoy [That is the way we do things]. The Russians' short, sharp explanation for everything, including the way you fold visas, is not open to question. Attempt to reason with them and they will respond, *Eto bylo by neporyadochno* [That would be improper]. End of conversation.

He meticulously refolded the visas and slid them

mechanically back into the passports the Russian way, and shoved them back through the glass slot. The officer distrustfully looked up and said, "Welcome to Moscow."

2
RUSSIANS
REDUNDANCY
AND RED TAPE

"What do we do next?" Robin said.

The passage through the passport/visa gate gave way to a baggage claim area filled with wall to wall people with little room left for luggage. We were about to discover another Russian custom; pushing, shoving, and crawling over others to get what you want, though impolite, is expected.

Everything looked old and run down. The conveyer belts that endlessly carried luggage to their respective owners had traveled far too many miles, straining with the rounding of every corner and grinding with every stop and start. The portable carts seemed to buckle under the weight of their burdens. The floors were filthy and unhealthy. Once we got into the queue and began to consider our next move, Lindsay decided to go into crawling mode and scooted off across the floor. She became instantly covered with dirt.

"Get up right now, little girl," I demanded while searching for the quickest method to retrieve our luggage. Lindsay got up and waddled back to us. She looked like one of the Moscow gypsy children, grimy from head to toe and smudged from ear to ear.

"Stay here while I get help," I said, pointing to the only empty bench in the area, and quickly ushering Robin, the kids and the carry-ons in that direction.

The cigarette smoke was so thick it burned our eyes. The noise was deafening. I could hardly carry on a conversation with Robin.

"I know we're supposed to fill out Customs papers," Robin said. "Why don't you ask someone where you get them?"

"I'll see what I can find out," I said. "It looks like our luggage hasn't started coming through yet."

I searched the area looking for any official-looking individuals. I saw none, so I started watching the crowd. Afraid to reveal my ignorance and insecurity, I nonchalantly scanned everyone around me. I noticed a large number of people huddled around a little stand filled with numerous cubbyholes. They were pushing and shoving against one another while attempting to snatch up pieces of paper.

I quickly stepped into the flow of the crowd and found myself right in the middle of the group grabbing at the pieces of paper. Eventually, I was able to get my hands on one. My suspicions were confirmed, it was the Customs Declaration. There was enough English on it for me to figure that out.

I looked back at Robin sitting on the broken down bench, seemingly helpless with all the carry-ons and two cranky children. The kids had been cooped up for the last ten hours. Lindsay had been awake for over eighteen hours which, for a two-year-old who is already prone to outbreaks of strong-willed behavior, spells nothing but trouble.

I knew Robin needed help. I knew that I had to fill out the Customs Declaration. I knew that the conveyor belt would start carrying our twelve oversized duffel bags through the hole in the wall at any moment. I knew that somehow I would have to get our luggage through Customs. I knew I needed help.

I had been told that someone would be waiting to meet us on the other side, but it was up to us to first get through Customs. I could see the long glass wall beyond the long, stagnant lines. Behind the glass, another endless mass of humanity was peering in, like children looking through the window of a candy store. I felt like we were on display. With Robin's bright, full-length turquoise winter coat and beautiful long blonde hair making her stick out like a sore thumb in the drab Russian crowd, that feeling intensified.

My preoccupation with all the things I needed to do was interrupted by a couple of scruffy-looking Russian men waving frantically, motioning me over to their desk. They looked friendly enough, so I moved in their direction hoping they wanted to help. I managed to keep a watchful eye on Robin, the kids, and the carry-ons as I made my way to the desk. We had been told to watch for thieves who would seek to take advantage of any opportunity, so I was wary.

"Help you, sir? Help you, sir?" the two men said. "Take your bags? Take your bags? Very cheap."

"Ah, sure. Come with me," I motioned. One man quickly grabbed his cart and followed.

I was willing to pay more than the normal rate, what-ever that was, just for the help. I waved at Robin, point-ing at the man following me, motioning that I was going to retrieve our luggage.

The conveyor belt had just started to creak and groan as we arrived at the pickup spot. The man motioned to me to show him which bags were mine. I tried to show him how many, but my hand gestures were a poor way to communicate in a crowded airport.

"There. There." I said, pointing to the first black duf-fel bag to come through. He wormed his way through the crowd, muscled the huge bag up to his hip with both hands and pulled it back through, nearly knocking over a couple of people in the process. He smiled and I nod-ded. He put the bag on the cart and started to wheel it off, motioning for me to follow him.

"No, no," I said. "More, more," pointing back to the conveyor belt.

"Here's another . . . and another . . . and another." I, too, learned how to maneuver in the crowd, grab a bag, and duck back out. I was a little more considerate of those standing in the way than my Russian helper, but I still bumped a few.

After the fifth duffel bag, my helper realized that he had gotten in over his head. He turned and walked off shaking his head. I couldn't believe it. I had five bags on the one cart with no more room to spare, each weighing between sixty-five and seventy pounds, and I still had seven more bags to go. I was quickly becoming disillusioned and losing all hope. I was also concerned with how Robin was holding up. I had temporarily lost sight of her while concentrating on my current project.

Then, to my surprise and relief, my Russian helper returned with another man and two more carts. He appeared to be in better spirits, ready to tackle more luggage.

I learned another custom. Russians often exit unannounced and then return with the necessary tools to handle the situation. They don't ask. They don't inform. They just do it.

I quickly pointed out the next seven bags. We went through the same ritual with each retrieval; push and shove, shove and push. The three carts loaded with our oversized duffel bags seemed to give under the weight. He motioned for me to lead the way while he and his friend maneuvered the three carts. Each man would push a cart ten feet, then go back and grab another one and push it ten feet past the first one. Both men worked all three carts like a well-oiled machine. It was the first sign of sensible order I had seen since arriving.

"Robin," I shouted over the crowd trying to get her attention. Seth heard me, saw me, jumped up and began to run toward me, darting back and forth under and around bags being toted by the crowd. Robin yelled for Seth to stay put, but it was too late.

He jumped into my arms as if I had been gone a long time. "Let's not do that again," I said. "You could get lost in here and I don't know what I'd do if I couldn't find you."

"Okay, Daddy, but I just wanted to hug you," he said, latching tightly on to me, overcome with all the new faces and strange surroundings.

The two men finally strong-armed the carts up to where we were and looked in disbelief at our eight over-sized carry-ons. I motioned that we needed to load these as well. One man disappeared, shaking his head again, but this time I knew he would return, probably with another cart.

When he returned, the two men quickly loaded the eight bags and then began to point at the numerous long lines through Customs. I attempted to take charge of one of the carts and lead the way. One of the men quick-ly pried it out of my hands and assured me with hand motions that they would take care of it.

"Which line do we get in?" Robin said.

"Whichever is shortest," I replied. Everything appeared to be at a standstill. "I hope he's still there," I said, speaking of our contact we were supposed to meet. Two hours had already passed since our arrival.

"I'm sure he'll be here somewhere," Robin said.

I looked at the two men and shrugged my shoulders, not knowing exactly what to do. They sensed my indecision and took charge. They began to inch us toward a Customs gate that looked like it was closed. The whole fiasco looked like a long wagon train. Those stuck in the long lines looked on with envy. They seemed to know what was going to happen.

Great, I thought, *is this where we get the opportunity to bribe a Customs Official?* I had told myself that I would never succumb to this type of personal attention.

One of the men disappeared through the gate and quickly returned with another young man in a Russian uniform. He motioned for us to quickly begin making our way to the gate while his buddy concentrated on moving all four carts, one at a time.

The Customs Official was pleasant looking, though he looked like he had just graduated from high school. His oversized uniform added to the impression and I found his childlike face to be incongruous with the authority of his position.

"Customs Papers, please?" the young Customs Officer said, holding out his hand.

I hastily reached into my pocket and pulled out the crumpled form. It was blank. I turned to Robin and asked for a pen. I looked down at the paper and attempted to decipher what information it wanted. The young officer seemed like he wanted to help.

"Do you have anything to declare?" he said in a surprising tone of authority.

"What do you mean?" I said.

"What do you have in your luggage?"

"Clothes, toiletries, and medicines."

"Any weapons or drugs?"

"No."

"How long will you be in Moscow?"

"For at least one year," I said.

"Are you here on business or pleasure?" he said.

"Business."

"How much money do you have with you?"

I pondered a moment thinking it might be the set-up for a bribe, and then decided that the truth would be the best answer.

"Eight-hundred dollars." I spoke with hesitancy as if I suspected he was going to ask for it all.

"Write that amount right here," the young man pointed to a particular line. "And on this line, write how much luggage you have with you," he continued.

I frantically filled out the information and then handed the document to him.

The young officer looked puzzled, and then said, "Where is your wife and children's Customs Declaration papers?"

I looked back to the spot where I had fought for my papers hours before and saw that it was just as crowded.

The young man sensed my despair and reached behind the counter and pulled out a handful of blank documents and handed three of them to me. I was going to have to fill one out for our two-year-old as well, but I was not in a position to debate the issue. So I began writing as quickly as possible.

I had to readjust my baggage declaration on my own form in order to spread out the number of bags among the four of us. I also had to readjust the money declaration and declare some on Robin's form.

The two men assisting us were waiting, but seemed very impatient, surveying the crowd as if they were attempting to avoid being caught. I chose not to ask any questions. I couldn't anyway, I had no idea if what I was doing was legal or not. No one else seemed to care, except those trapped in the long lines.

I handed the completed documents back to the young man. He stamped all of them firmly and repeatedly. I would soon learn that any document or piece of paper in Russia, no matter how small and insignificant, is useless unless it has been stamped. You could have papers with Mickey Mouse's face stamped all over them validating their authenticity and you wouldn't have a problem, just as long as they had been stamped.

The young officer handed the documents back to me. "You must keep these documents with you and bring them back when you leave Moscow."

I really didn't know if the yellowing paper on which the documents had been printed would last that long. It looked and felt very old and brittle.

The young officer then opened the Customs gate, smiled and said, "Welcome to Moscow."

He didn't ask for money. He didn't even hint for a tip, and I really don't think he would have accepted one. My suspicions were squelched and my confidence was bolstered. Not everyone in Customs was crooked, as I had been led to believe from more experienced travelers in this part of the world.

This welcome seemed more inviting than the one received a couple of hours earlier.

"Excuse me," I shouted, elbowing my way through the dense crowd, attempting to cut a swath for my family. I guess I should have let the two men handling our baggage lead the way. Our duffel bags were about forty inches long which, when placed sideways on a cart, would have cleared a path through the crowd wide enough for all four of us.

"Look for our name," Robin said pointing to the long line of people holding up signs and posters with names on them. Some names were scribbled on pieces of cardboard, while others had been printed with elaborate fonts on laser printers. Some were even in color. One sign caused me to do a double-take. Under the man's name, written in big bold letters was "Delta Airlines® Dream Vacations." I couldn't believe it was a dream vacation destination.

Everyone had flowers, bouquets of every color. No matter what the event, Russians bring flowers.

As we were slowly walking down the line, carefully examining each sign, we could feel ourselves being inspected just as closely by the bearers of the signs. Most of the men standing around wore either black or brown leather coats dulled by the resin of their cigarette smoke. The only bright colors in the place were the flowers and Robin's bright turquoise coat. Nearly everyone wore some type of a hat or a *shapka* [winter hat].

"There it is." I pointed while grabbing Robin's hand and moving forward, making sure that she had hold of both Seth and Lindsay. "Boy, am I glad to see you." I stuck my hand out while uttering a sigh of relief.

"I am Misha," the young man said with a broad smile, shaking my hand firmly.

"I'm Rick and this is my wife Robin."

Misha offered Robin a bouquet of flowers. She cheerfully received them as a breath of fresh air.

"I will take your bags," Misha volunteered. I turned around and motioned the two men to come forward.

"Oh my," he said. "So many bags. And I have a little car."

"What should we do?" I said.

"I will rent two cars here and they will take your bags to the hotel," Misha said. "It will cost about twenty-five dollars per car. Is that okay?"

"Sure."

I asked Misha what the two helpers should be paid. He spoke with them briefly and seemed to strike a deal. Russian is a very rough, guttural language which makes it sound like people are arguing with one another when they're actually getting along quite well.

"Twenty-five dollars," he said.

After all they had done, I was surprised they didn't ask for more.

"I will take Robin and the children to the car," Misha explained. "It is very cold and my car is warm. You must stay here with the luggage while I hire the taxis."

He quickly exited with Robin, Seth and Lindsay firmly attached to one another. There I stood, exposed and self conscious about the number of bags I had to guard and the number of men appearing to size me up in this vulnerable situation. Every direction I looked I saw three or four men huddled closely together glancing over their shoulders at me and mumbling among themselves, while puffing on their cigarettes and attempting to stay warm each time the doors opened.

I had been warned not to leave my baggage unattended in *Sheremetyevo II*, particularly while in that section of the airport. Thieves would grab a bag, any bag, rush outdoors, jump into a waiting car and speed away.

At last, Misha walked back through the doors and instructed the men to bring the bags outside. All four of us grabbed a cart and maneuvered them outside. There were three men waiting for us, all in dark leather jackets barking at one another while shifting gas cans and other assorted things around in their trunks, making room for the bags. Their cars were black *Volgas*, the kind KGB Agents drive in movies.

I shook the hands of both men who had helped us through the ordeal. I paid the twenty-five-dollar fee and gave each of them a five-dollar tip, attempting to express how much I appreciated their help. They seemed embarrassed and cautious. They looked around to see if anyone was looking on, which there were, took the money, shoved it into their pockets and disappeared.

Misha told me to go ahead and get in the car with Robin and the kids. I gladly accepted his suggestion. It was the first time I had sat down since we had gotten off the jet, and suddenly I realized how tired I was. The car was warm and the kids were nearly asleep in Robin's arms, totally exhausted. It had been some twenty hours since they had laid in a bed. The plush seat of the late model Volvo® did feel good.

I looked out and noticed it had stopped snowing. A few minutes later, Misha jumped in the car and said, "Let's go."

3
THE SIGHTS
THE SOUNDS
AND THE SOMBERNESS

Sheremetyevo II is located in the northern outskirts of Moscow, mostly surrounded by farmland. The drive into central Moscow would take some forty-five minutes. I learned that Misha had been a European racecar driver and it quickly became apparent that he had not lost his desire nor his technique for handling fast cars.

I immediately noticed the high speed at which everyone drove. It surprised me that though Misha's car was much newer than the Volgas carrying our luggage, they quickly left us behind, disappearing up in the distance. The streets were clear of snow, yet very wet and dirty. Misha could hardly keep his windshield clear of the thick black muck thrown up from cars passing us. This added to the adventure of darting in and out of traffic without sideswiping another speeder. I found myself clinging to anything within reach as Misha sped along.

The frozen countryside transformed into an overcrowded landscape of flats of all shapes and sizes. State-run stores seemed to occupy the first floor of each building.

There were a few late model cars on the streets, but most of the traffic was made up of older vehicles which displayed the cruelty of Moscow winters. The traffic was becoming more and more congested which made Misha's mission to get us to the hotel in a timely fashion even more challenging.

He turned down darkened, nameless side streets as shortcuts. We found ourselves going the wrong way down one way streets for short distances as needed. We sent a good number of pedestrians running for cover as they chanced crossing the street in front us. Misha flashed his brights at another car only one time as he was passing them, but he was constantly flashing pedestrians, offering a polite warning to get out of the way. Most of them heeded the advice.

After a few more close calls, it was clear Misha was adept at navigating through Moscow traffic. White stripes and yellow lines mean nothing to the *Muscovite*. I suspect they were only to give the city crews something to do, though the time spent coloring the streets could have been put to better use on street repair. We didn't go down a single street without potholes or huge portions of caved in asphalt. It was just as challenging to navigate around the crumbling streets as it was the traffic.

The Stalin buildings, nicknamed the Sister buildings,

were quite impressive. Misha explained to us that there were seven of them strategically placed around the city and that you could see each of the other six from any one of them. The jagged structure and looming towers protruding into the night sky seemed ominous, almost evil, in comparison to the otherwise ordinary lines of the surrounding architecture. Lindsay would later refer to these Stalin buildings as "The Castles."

The hotel was a welcome sight. It was poised on the Moscow River offering a brief glimpse of a modern metropolis with its spotlights pointing upward, brightly illuminating its name for all to see.

I had been hired as a Project Manager for a Russian company who was committed to turning a portion of their four-star hotel into an American style business center. The plan was to offer a Western environment for Western businessmen who preferred the creature comforts of home while doing business in Eastern Europe. I didn't know exactly what my job description would be, but I was assured there was plenty of work to be done. My contract offered me and my family a room at the hotel for three weeks. After that, we were expected to move into a Russian flat and become "Russianized."

4
THE FUTURE
THE FAILURE
AND THE FEARS

The hotel room was dark and quiet except for the hushed drone of a heating station off in the distance. A dull gray haze filtered through the hotel drapes. Laying there in bed, a surge of memories began to flood my thoughts. I rubbed my eyes, wondering if it had just been a dream. I looked down at Lindsay and Seth. They hadn't moved from the position they were in the night before. I looked over at Robin. She was also motionless. I was tempted to reach over and wake her and begin talking of our future and assessing what had happened thus far. Here we were, in another country thousands of miles from friends and family. I wanted the assurance that I had made the right choice for my family, but all I could do was lay there. I let Robin sleep.

We now live in Moscow, I thought. *We really live in Moscow.* There were new sights, new neighbors, new opportunities, and new ways of doing things.

Thoughts came crashing in. *Have I just made the biggest mistake of my life,* I questioned myself. *I've dragged my wife and kids halfway around the world.*

We had received all sorts of free advice from people who had visited Russia. Many were self-proclaimed experts whom I think were more interested in listening to themselves talk of their escapades than helping us prepare to live cross-culturally. Their advice offered often came as warnings:

"Watch out for Gypsies. Their children will steal you blind."

"Don't drink the water. The parasites will make you sick."

"Avoid the train stations. Hoodlums and thugs hang out there."

"Don't use public restrooms. They're filthy and they never have toilet paper."

"Don't speak English on the Metro. Many Russians hate Americans."

"Always carry mace with you. Be prepared when a mugger approaches you."

"Don't go to a *Poly Clinic.* The needles are unsterile and carry disease."

"Don't buy rubles on the street. They're probably counterfeit."

"Don't take a taxi. They'll cheat you blind."

The warnings were reactive and rooted in distrust. It was a typical response to a society these people knew little about, and preferred to keep at arms length. Perhaps they had a fear of revealing that Russians are not really that different from us, relatively speaking. Then their tales would seem less dramatic and sensational.

As I laid there, I knew I was going to have to make some proactive decisions. We were expected to be assimilated into Russian society in three weeks or less. *But how would we do it?* We had no car, no driver. No map for bus routes. No tokens for the Metro. No knowledge of how to get around the city.

We had no idea how we were going to shop for food. *Where would we exchange our dollars for rubles?* We didn't know where or how we would live. *What was considered a good residential area in Moscow? How expensive would it be? What about utilities? Would I have to take the Metro to work every day? What about Seth's school next September? Where was Lindsay going to play? What if one of us became ill or was injured and had to go to the hospital? What would Robin do during the day? Where could we go to Church?*

The city of Moscow doesn't provide Yellow Pages, much less White Pages. I later found out that much of their current phone system was still pre-World War I. With service like that, they didn't really need Yellow Pages. You rarely get the same flat twice when you dial the same phone number. Dialing is the luck of the draw in Moscow. We would have to rely upon our own ingenuity for networking.

As reality began to sink in, I suspected I had gotten us in over our heads. All I knew was that both Robin and I felt we were supposed to go to Russia.

I sat up, reached for the drapes and pushed them back. The gray day didn't brighten the dark paneled room. We were on the fifth floor of the hotel, and we had a view opposite the Moscow River. In other words, we were on the back side of the hotel. I saw two huge smoke stacks with steam billowing out and becoming one with the clouds. It was the heating station for this portion of the city. We would soon learn the purpose of these centralized heating stations, but at that point the distant drone of the plant only added to the despair of it all.

I could see a long, narrow brown building full of flats parallel to the hotel. It was outlined by a road circling the building. Cars were parked everywhere. There were no garages and no driveways to be found. Anywhere there was a space the night before was filled with a car that morning.

The fresh snow from the evening before was already turning brown. Everything seemed dead and motionless. There was a lone grandmother, known in Russia as a *babushka*, leaning against a chainlink fence that surrounded a tiny playground. She was watching her grandchild play on the lone swing. The playground, designated for that particular flat, was nothing more than a swing and a slide on a piece of frozen ground. I wondered what the little *babushka's* life must have been like. She must have been there during Stalin, and had seen the fall of Communism, I thought. From my vantage point, she looked tired and worn out, using the fence as her crutch.

I looked at my watch. It was 9:00 a.m., Saturday morning. Work would not start until Monday so I had two days to think through our plans, though despair was quickly mounting, making me feel immobile. I tried to fight the feeling of helplessness, but the task before us seemed so immense.

I laid back down. The winter sight was overwhelming. *Moving here in the summer would have been easier*, I thought. I couldn't share that with Robin, though. She seemed so confident and sure that we were going to make it. Little did I know that she was experiencing the same questions and emotions I was feeling.

I turned over and went back to sleep, hoping that things would somehow be different the next time I awoke.

5
RENTING
RENEGING
AND RENEGOTIATING

"It reads, 'Russian Flat with Western Style right on the Moscow River,'" Robin said, reading the classifieds in one of the two English newspapers available in the hotel.

"That sounds promising," I said. "Let's call them and see where it is and how much it costs."

I was relieved to see a familiar looking newspaper.

"It's interesting. They have a phone number for English-speaking people and a phone number for Russian-speaking people," Robin said.

I dialed the number and received a curt, *"Ah-low."*

"Uh, hello, my name is Rick Fur--" I said before being cut off. "Hmm. We must have been disconnected. I'll try again."

"Ah-low," came the terse tone once again.

"Yes, my name is Rick Furmanek and we're inter--"

Russians answer the phone with a brisk *"Ah-low,"* as

if they're late for an appointment and have no time to talk. If they don't understand the caller, or don't wish to speak with them, they simply hang up the phone. They don't say a thing; they just hang up. Anything different would not be proper.

"I guess it was a wrong number. Do you see any more in there?" I said.

"Yes, try this one." Robin handed me the paper with an ad circled and another English-speaking number.

"Hello," the Slavic voice answered.

"Hello. I saw your ad in the newspaper for a flat that has been recently remodeled. Do you still have it for rent?"

"Yes, it is still for rent." The voice seemed friendly enough.

"How much are you asking for it?"

"Three-thousand five-hundred per month to be paid in quarters, up front, with the last month's rent and a one-thousand dollar deposit. It is very cheap for such a nice flat."

"Excuse me, did you say three-thousand five-hundred per month?"

"Yes. It is very nice with lots of new furniture. It has many rooms."

"Thank you very much," I said as I hung up the phone. "I think we underestimated how much it would cost to live here. They want three-thousand five-hundred per month."

"You've got to be kidding," Robin said

Each ad produced the same overpriced responses with the trailer, "It is very good price. Very cheap."

I learned that Moscow was the most expensive city to live in throughout Europe, and the fifth most expensive city to live in throughout the entire world.

There were some flats a little cheaper -- twelve to fifteen-hundred -- which could be paid for on a monthly schedule. Then there were these smaller ads that read something like, "We will find you a good flat. You name the price and location. Many selections to choose from. Call Olga . . . or Yelena . . . or Oxana . . . or Sveta today!"

"Let me see what the other ex-pats are doing when I go in Monday," I said. "I'll ask around and see if we can get any help."

The next day, I found that renting a flat wasn't impossible once I learned who to ask. Our company had retained the services of a flat finder. I figured I could ask my secretary and translator to call her and set up an appointment since Robin and I had gotten nowhere in the Classifieds.

A time was set for us to meet Lena, our flat finder, in front of our hotel the next day. I had given her our price range -- substantially less than what we saw in the paper -- and gave her very basic requirements: a bathroom that worked and a steel front door. We could make do without the other amenities if necessary.

I had been forewarned that a steel door was essential for foreigners. Thieves would merely kick in another type of door and a steel one at least slowed them down a bit so you could call the *Militsiya*. If an ex-patriate rents a flat without one, they are encouraged to get one as quickly as possible. Word gets around when an *Amerikanski* [American] moves into a building. Some become easy targets for the growing number of mafia gangs. Some become the target for the steel door sales-man. One couple we got to know had purchased three steel doors before they figured out that the company was actually installing them in such a way that they could return later, preferably late at night, and steal the door back, then resell it to someone else. Our friends learned their lesson on the third door and finally hired a company that had been in business longer than six months, and had references other than Boris and Uri -- probably brothers-in-law.

The next day we met Lena as arranged, and went through the formal introductions. Her English was good, so we felt comfortable that she could understand our needs. Financially speaking, we knew a Western-style flat was out of the question. Anyway, we wanted to live as much like a Russian family as possible, we thought we should strive for that true cultural experi-ence. Now we were being forced to do so.

Our first stop took us to a suburb of Moscow, well known for its parks and forests, called *Sokolniki*. Though it was early in the evening, it was already dark. Because Moscow is as far north as the middle of the Hudson Bay, darkness arrives by late afternoon in mid-March. We would be unable to see any of the parks or forests, yet Lena assured us that this was a place that was very desirable. Our children could have a place to play and it was close to a Metro station for easy travel.

The *Sokolniki* Metro is located near a large intersection that proved both interesting and saddening. Coming up out of the Metro, the spotty lighting illumined a sizable, hurried crowd of ghost-like shadows scurrying home with plastic shopping bags and oversized parcels. Their demeanor was not one of excitement or even frustration, but rather one of resignation.

There were *kiosks* lining the streets in every direction. A Russian *kiosk* is a small portable building about eight feet square, offering anything from cigarettes and perfume to canned meat. If you don't like what you see in the window of one *kiosk,* you move on to the next one. It is the Russian entrepreneur's launching pad. If you could live with the mafia's demand for protection money, then you might just make it. It appeared that it was the mafia's job to protect you from organized crime, and for the right price, you'd get it.

The large intersection was interesting because you could see all types of people in one location. It was also depressing because you could see all types of people. It was the first time I had ever seen Russians too drunk to stand. They leaned on one another while they stumbled down the street trying to help each other get home.

"Is so sad," said Lena, shaking her head slowly. She

seemed embarrassed by the sight and she quickly changed the subject. "The place you will see is very nice and it is very cheap for an American."

I heard the word "cheap" in almost every conversation I ever had there concerning money. There seemed to be a prevailing misconception that all Americans are rich. They thought my protestation was only modesty and refused to believe that there was poverty in America.

Finally, the building which housed the flat in question was in sight. It was about two blocks from the Metro, but that evening it seemed a bit further. It was located down a dark street with huge piles of worn-out snow long since turned to ice covering both sidewalks, forcing us to walk in the road. The chemicals used on the streets during the winter turned the road into a slushy mess which was impossible to maneuver around. Our feet became cold and wet. This being our first adventure outside the hotel, we still had not prepared properly for the outing.

"Here it is," Lena said, pointing to an entrance protected by a large cracked and peeling wooden door. "The people are very nice and they want to rent the flat to you."

"Can you lock this entrance at night?" I said, skeptically eyeing the door.

"Some buildings have entrances that lock and the tenants use an intercom from their flat to let people in," she said. "This building used to have one, but it was broken

by the tenants long ago. Many Russians prefer not dealing with locked entrances, especially when they come
home drunk, and they break the lock so it will not work
again. If you need an entrance that has a lock and is
functioning properly, that will be more money."

The entrance into the building opened into a dimly lit
hallway. It was lined with chipped and discolored tile,
eroded from years of neglect. The nauseating mixture of
cigarette smoke, vodka, and urine assaulted our senses.
At first impression, I had decided to rule the flat out, but
I still wanted to see what was so great about it and why
Lena was so insistent that we take it.

The building did not have an elevator, so we began
climbing the many stairs to the fifth floor. I tried to
imagine Robin carrying armload's of groceries up all the
stairs, all the while urging the children, for an entire
year. It wasn't a pretty thought. Each floor we climbed
revealed a flat's dinner menu for that evening. The
greasy smell of fried cabbage and potatoes mixing with
the already pungent odors wafting throughout the
building was almost more than we could stomach.

At the fifth floor, we came to a steel door padded
with maroon leather-looking vinyl shaped in tiny diamond patterns. She rang the doorbell and I heard someone on the other side opening the door; at least, I
thought they were opening the door. I heard locks turning and chains clanging and finally a door opening, but
the door I was looking at hadn't budged. Finally I heard
a loud clank and the huge steel door swung open reveal-

ing another smaller door, inset with multiple locks on it.

A thin, pale looking young man greeted Lena in Russian. Pulling the cigarette out of his mouth with his thumb and middle finger, he greeted us with a smile. His family was already seated in the miniature kitchen around a dwarfed kitchen table eating their dinner. The wife smiled, quickly stood and began pointing to various items in the kitchen: the refrigerator, the stove, the sink, and the cabinets. Later we found out that even owning some of these things was a luxury to many Russians.

"All this can be yours," Lena offered with a smile. "They want to leave you their knives, forks, spoons, plates, dishes and some of their food. All their bed sheets, their black and white Russian TV, and books too."

I wasn't sure if Lena and this family expect us to rent it on the spot and bed down for the night. The pungent odor of something pickled coming from a small closet added to the uneasiness that was building in me.

"How large is this?" I said. "Could we see the rest of the flat?" I half expected to find the family's suitcases already packed in another room. They seemed ready to vacate in a moment's notice.

"Yes, of course," Lena said.

The young man led the way into the main room while Lena was describing all the things that they were going to leave, which was everything we saw.

"They will go live with their sister," Lena said.

"Many Russians will rent their own flat for a good price and then move in with their relatives while theirs is occupied. It is very uncomfortable, but this is the Russian way of renting a flat."

"How many live in a flat together?" I said.

"Oh, two, maybe three families. But this is the way it is done."

All the furniture was veneered with a glossy reddish finish, a fifties post-modern style. Everything was either in duplicate or triplicate, there were no vacant spaces on the walls or the floors. Everywhere you looked there was either a bookcase, a china case, or a Persian rug. Even if we wanted to buy furniture, we wouldn't have any room for it.

One quick glance through each of the tiny rooms confirmed that it wasn't the place for us. Even with the offer of stained pillows and used up bath towels, it just didn't feel quite right. Maybe it was the filth of the floors. Maybe it was the ancient fixtures throughout the flat. Maybe it was the thirty-watt light bulbs hanging from a single cord in each room offering a dim view of everything. Maybe it was the mysterious meat laying out on the window sill. Maybe it was the foul odor from the clothes worn that day, airing out for the next day's work on the makeshift clothesline over the bathtub.

We thanked the family and wished them well, hoping within that they weren't as disillusioned as we were. Our first experience had not been too promising. We headed back to the hotel, wishing that we could just stay there and not have to worry about finding a flat. We had been told to prepare mentally to live internationally. If we had been expecting the creature comforts of the West in Moscow, we would have been sorely disappointed on our first outing, but we knew that there had to be a flat out there somewhere that would meet our needs. We had checked our wants back at the hotel. We decided we would meet again on Saturday morning and see some more flats.

Lena, Olga, our newfound friend and chauffeur for the day, and Alla, our acquaintance turned friend and confidante, had agreed to meet us at the prearranged rendezvous spot in front of the hotel. We would grab a quick breakfast at the hotel restaurant and be ready and waiting when they showed up.

The kids seemed to like the young Russian girl we had hired, a family friend of Olga's, to watch them while we combed the streets for a flat. Sveta, the sitter, seemed trustworthy and friendly and was good with the kids.

The only struggle we were experiencing was becoming weary of going to the same restaurant for breakfast, lunch and dinner. We didn't have a choice at this time, living in the hotel, and the menu was extremely limited. At first glance, the buffet looked wonderful, but buffets cooked in two inches of butter under the influence of the French chef, three times a day seven days a week, were wearing on all of us. Even the two a la carte items of spaghetti and hamburgers were getting old. We needed a change and it couldn't come too soon.

Lena, Olga and Alla greeted us with the typical Russian greeting, three alternating kisses on the cheeks, from each person. We climbed into Olga's little *Lada* and headed to the west part of the city.

"Many diplomats live in these buildings," Lena pointed to the row of high-rise flats lining the street. "They are very new and very nice."

Peering out of the tiny back seat of the *Lada* I could see high-rise after high-rise surrounded by frozen dirt now turned into black sludge from the warming temperatures. There were no lawns or trees.

The thick, outer walls of each high-rise building seemed to be the only thing that prevented Russians from parking their cars in their own living rooms. Cars were parked everywhere, parallel, diagonally, straight, and cockeyed. They were backed in, forced in, pried in and boxed in, and they were as dirty as the muck they rested upon. Some men were out on the bright, sunny Saturday morning making a feeble attempt to wash the crud off their autos from the night before. They would make a dozen trips back and forth to and from the flat for relatively clean water to wash the car. There are no water faucets to be found outside, the frozen Russian winters would not allow them.

The muddy playground surround by a wobbly chain link fence was full of children bundled so tightly from head to toe they looked like little stone statues waddling back and forth from one swing to the next.

"At least the children would have a playground here," Robin said, encouraged at the sight.

"Here we are," Lena said to our driver Olga, as she jumped the curb and slid into a spot. "Watch your step, it is very wet and slippery."

We were prepared this time, we had our snow boots on. We made our way around to the back entrance of the building and opened the heavy door revealing a large gray concrete hallway. The door looked old, but it wasn't broken, cracked or peeling.

The odor was the same, vodka, cigarettes and urine. We couldn't escape it.

"Oh this is very nice. The hallways are so large," Alla said with envy. "You should move here. This is all so new. It will be very good for you."

Maybe it was the bright sunshine of the morning that put us in a more optimistic mood, but I felt good about the day ahead.

"They have nice elevators," Lena pointed out. "This family is on the nineteenth floor."

"What do they do in case of a fire?" I said.

"There is not much you can do from the nineteenth floor," she said and quickly changed the subject.

"Here we are." The elevator door opened, revealing a large door blocking the entrance into the hallway. It was barricaded with a keypad lock on it. "This is very secure. You must have the owner's permission to get beyond this door. It is very safe," Lena assured us.

"But what about a fire?" I said again.

The intercom responded, *"Da?"*

Lena informed the family that we were there to see the flat. They quickly unbolted their doors and came out to meet us. The family seemed very happy to see us although they couldn't speak a word of English.

All we could say was, *"Ochin Priyatnah"* [Pleased to meet you].

"This has four rooms," Lena said as we entered the flat.

Four rooms means a living room and three bedrooms, or perhaps a living room, dining room and two bedrooms which was the case at that apartment. They never count kitchens or bathrooms as rooms because they were more like closets in the flats we visited.

A teenage boy came out of his room smiling from ear to ear and secretly motioned for me to come in. I consented with a smile in return and followed him into a room wallpapered with pornography.

"You like?" he said with a grin while offering me a cigarette. "You can keep."

"Uh, no thank you on both points," I said declining with hand motions.

He shrugged his shoulders and quickly exited the flat.

Robin was showing verbal signs of approval when she and the other women entered the teenager's room. Embarrassed, I quickly exited to look for a more positive sign that we should rent the place. The women exited the teenager's room just as quickly and without a word. I think the mother was embarrassed as well.

"Do you like it?" Lena said.

"It has potential," Robin said.

"Good," Lena said excitedly.

She turned to the couple and started asking more questions in Russian. The discussion soon developed an air of tension.

"It is not good," Alla whispered.

"What's going on?" I said.

"They want more money now that you like it," she said.

"How much more?"

"Two-hundred American dollars more a month."

"Tell them no," I said. "They agreed to rent it for this price and we can't afford to pay any more. Please tell them that. And you might as well ask them what a person is supposed to do on the nineteenth floor in case of a fire too." I was feeling the tension as I listened to the tone of the discussion. Smiles quickly turned to stoicism.

"I think they will rent it to another person," Lena sighed.

"Is this how Russians deal with lease agreements and advertising?" I said.

"I think they think you are a rich American and can afford more money for such a nice flat."

"We can't and that is that."

We thanked the couple and said our goodbyes and

headed out the door.

We slid out of our parking spot and over the curb in silence. Finally, back on the main road leading into downtown Moscow, Lena said, "I think they were difficult people and not very honest. I have one other flat we can look at. It is near the University. Perhaps this one will not be difficult."

I prayed that the third would be the charm. We only had two more weeks to find a flat and time was passing by quickly.

Sitting atop Sparrow Hills, formerly known as Lenin Hills, Moscow University, with its Stalin era spire architectural influence, overlooks the Moscow River and *Luzhniki* Stadium. The long ski jump, also at the top of the hill, built as a practice facility for the 1980 Olympics, gives the illusion that those brave enough to make the trek down the hill would end up smack dab in the middle of the Moscow River. The scenic overlook attracts many tourists and provides an ideal place for souvenir hunters and gatherers.

It's also a popular spot for outdoor weddings. The tradition for many Russian couples is to have their wedding on the hill, and after their vows take a horse-drawn carriage up and down the street. Then they travel with friends to the Grave of the Unknown Soldier and place flowers on the Memorial. Last they are driven home to participate in a huge wedding party, lasting two or three days. It is a great tradition for the Russian people. The tragedy is that it is just as popular a tradition to get a divorce as it is to have a wedding in Moscow.

On the way to the appointment, Lena pointed out the New Circus, housed in a large circular building, which ran nearly every night of the year. The kids would enjoy it. The Metro was close by and there were numerous markets a short bus or trolley ride away. There was also the Young Communists' Headquarters, the equivalent of the Boy Scouts of America, only they taught young Russians unfavorable ideas about the great Imperialists living in the U.S.

We turned down *Krupskaya* and found the street to be lined with shorter ten story buildings. The street was very beautiful with the evergreens filling out the boulevard. There were children everywhere.

"Lenin's wife was named *Krupskaya*. This is the street named after her. He loved her very much," Lena said.

At the end of the street was a statue in the boulevard with Lenin and *Krupskaya* sitting on a park bench. Russians seemed to look for any excuse to build a statue. They take great pride in their history, especially their leaders, writers and poets.

We turned off *Krupskaya* onto a narrow one-way street that circled the building.

"See, you have two playgrounds and a grade school with a playground. This will be very safe for your children," Lena said. "Many families who attend the University live in these flats."

We slid to a stop, up and over the curb. I noticed a huge cloud of steam billowing up through a gaping hole in the ground that was large enough to swallow up a little car like ours. "What is that?" I said.

"It looks as if the hot water line has broken and the ground has caved in around it," Olga said nonchalantly as if this were a regular occurrence.

"Much of our sewer and water system is broken in Moscow. Everything seems to fall apart," Lena said.

The door to the entrance looked all too familiar, cracked, peeling and broken. The intercom had long since been disassembled and probably sold at the local hardware market.

"This residence was built during the time of Stalin," Lena said. "The walls are very thick and it is very sturdy." Although I noticed the bricks protruding substantially toward the top of the outer wall, giving the appearance that they could give way at any time, I would have to trust Lena's knowledge of Russian construction.

Stepping into the hallway, the odor was familiar except for the slight odor of dirty water. The cleaning woman had just come out of the elevator backwards slinging a filthy mop back and forth, not caring whom she might whack in the process. She had started on the tenth floor with a clean bucket of water and was finishing up on the first floor with the leftovers. She had not changed the water once, nor did it appear that she had changed her clothes in a long, long time. Bent over, cracked and withered, performing this back-breaking job every day of washing floors, stairs and elevators had taken its toll on her. She didn't even look up to see who it was.

"The flat is on the fourth floor," Lena said. "Yelena seems to be a very nice woman and desires to rent the flat to an American family with children."

The elevator was encased in an old steel cage, but seemed to run smoothly. The familiar smell of the vodka was dulled by the recent mop job, but the urine odor was still pungent.

The elevator doors opened, revealing a small, narrow hallway going left and right. The discolored tile lining the walls and the floor reflected some creativity in the design, though it was apparent they didn't have much to work with.

"These thick walls will protect you from the Russian winter," Lena commented. We nodded in appreciation of her wealth of information.

The doorbell let loose a loud, distorted sound, unpleasant to the ears. On the other side of the door came a muffled, "*Kto?* [Who?]"

Lena responded in Russian, informing the woman that we were there to see the flat. She quickly went to work on the inner door, unlocking bolt after bolt, chain lock after chain lock. Finally, I could hear the familiar creak of the inner door and a loud clank unlocking the outer door. A very large Russian woman, about fifty years old, stepped out into the hallway and greeted us. She had rosy cheeks, probably from too much salt, and a robust smile.

Yelena welcomed us into her flat. It looked old, but clean, even spotless. We could still smell the detergent in the air.

"Yelena wants to serve you some *chay* [tea] and cookies," Lena said. "It is a Russian custom for a friend to be invited into the kitchen for a cup of *chay*. I think she wants you to become her friend."

We gladly accepted the offer, even though I was anxious to get a look at the flat.

The kitchen was much larger than the ones we had seen earlier. There was even room for a medium-sized table. The previous kitchens had tiny tables out of necessity, they didn't have the luxury of worrying about the fit. Yelena explained through Lena that the stove and the refrigerator would stay, but the real prize she was offering was the Russian washing machine. It was about two feet tall and looked like it would hold two pairs of blue jeans at a time.

"Yelena wants to show you how it works," Lena said.

She explained that part of the wash was automatic, but at some point you were forced to get involved in the process. All the knobs were in Russian and there was no instruction booklet. Lena couldn't explain it. If we decided to lease the place, we were going to have to learn from trial and error.

Yelena pointed to the china we were drinking out of and told us that the entire set would stay along with the knives, forks, spoons, pots, pans and any food we might want. We nodded in appreciation of this now all too familiar offer.

We finished our tea and headed into the living room. It was a long room lined with that same glossy reddish veneered furniture and Persian rugs used as wallpaper. She indicated to us that the books and the Czechoslovakian crystal could stay for our enjoyment. She also pointed to the black and white TV and the two wardrobes standing in opposite corners as gifts of her generosity. It was crowded and somewhat gaudy to look at, but perhaps pleasant enough to live in.

She motioned to us to move into the smaller of the two bedrooms. She told Lena that this room would be for the kids. Lena had told her that we had a small boy and girl. She had some toys laying out indicating that they would be gifts for the children. There were two beds, one much smaller than the other, but just right for Lindsay. Things were looking good.

"There are a few things she would like to store here in the back of the kid's bedroom while she is living with her relatives, if that would be okay," Lena translated.

"No problem," I said. "Would it be okay if we told her what we did and didn't want to keep here in the flat?"

"There should not be a problem."

The other bedroom was quite large, but filled with more furniture and Persian rugs.

"Yelena has told me that if you rent this flat, she would like to fix up the bedroom for you," Lena explained.

"You really don't have to do that," Robin said.

"Oh, she insists," Lena said.

"Well, let's see the rest of the flat first," I said.

The bathroom was divided into two tiny rooms. One housed the bathtub and sink with makeshift clothesline and the other housed the toilet. I had seen this at the first flat and realized that it was the norm.

The toilet was ancient and its operation was not obvious. The toilet seat had been repaired so often with electrical tape that the once white plastic was now a shiny, sticky looking, black. It hurt just looking at it.

"Can she replace the toilet seat?" I said, not knowing if they were plentiful in Moscow or if she would have to order one.

"No problem," Lena translated. "Yelena would replace it within the first two weeks."

"Can Robin and I talk for a moment?" I said. Everyone quickly exited the room. "Hey, except for the toilet seat, it's the best one we've seen yet."

"I think it has potential," Robin said, truly encouraged.

"Okay Lena, tell her we'll take it," I said.

"Good. There's only one thing that must be done," Lena said.

"What is that?"

"We must talk Yelena down one-hundred dollars from her asking price unless you are willing to pay one-hundred dollars more per month?" Lena looked at me with hope.

"We just don't have it," I said. "We have decided on a budget for housing and that's all we can spend."

"Okay," Lena turned to Yelena and began bargaining.

Olga and Alla, who had been virtually silent the entire time, finally spoke up. "We think you ought to take it. It is old, but it is safe and the kids will have a wonderful playground to play in."

"Yelena wants to know how old your children are," Lena said.

"Two and five," Robin said.

Lena translated the answer and Yelena nodded in approval.

"She does not want your little ones to be on the streets of Moscow without anywhere to live so she would like you to come and live here for one-hundred dollars less per month," Lena informed us with a smile.

"Great, let's make it final now," I said.

"I have the documents here." Lena pulled out six handwritten copies of the contract, three in English and three in Russian. It only took her a few minutes to explain the process, but there seemed to be something fishy about the Russian contracts. Not reading Russian, we would have to trust Lena with the lease arrangements. She quickly filled in the blank spots with the dollar figures on the English contracts and entered the ruble amount on the Russian contracts. We all signed on the dotted line as if there was an urgent deadline to meet.

Once our signatures were on paper, we all looked up and breathed a sigh of relief, but for different reasons we would find out later.

It was agreed that we would meet the next week with the deposit and the first month's rent and to collect the keys. We thanked Yelena and quickly exited before anyone had the chance to change their minds. We had leased our first Russian flat.

"Be thankful you didn't rent the high-rise," my boss, the Company's General Manager, counseled me. "Two things you want to avoid when looking for a flat. Number one, don't rent anything on the first floor. It's easy for thieves to break a window, climb in and carry off your belongings. Steel bars over the windows often do not help. So never rent on the first floor. Number two," he continued, "avoid buildings that have more than ten stories. Too many people, too many opportunists, too dangerous in case of a fire."

6
MICE
MEN
AND METROS

Many tourists visiting Moscow consider a ride on the Metro under the Ring Road a highpoint of their sightseeing adventure. Most residents living in Moscow consider a ride on the Metro a necessary evil. Like cattle cars destined for the local stockyards, every few minutes Metro cars are crammed with vast herds of people carting them off to fulfill their duty as a citizen of Moscow. Transporting over eight and one-half million people each day, yet receiving very little attention with regards to maintenance, the Moscow Metro, once known for its grandeur, architecture and artwork, exhibited the signs of neglect.

Built in a circular fashion reflecting the Ring Road above, with the Kremlin at its center, the Metro is one of the few modes of transportation in Russia that was on time, barring any unforeseen disaster. Like clockwork, the Metro trains circle the city traveling in opposite directions simultaneously, on separate tracks, making it convenient to journey to another portion of the city and back in a relatively short period of time.

You may exit your Metro car at any station, move to another level and be transported to the far reaches of the city. The palm of a hand was like the Ring Road, circular in nature, and the fingers were the various Metro lines extending out in different directions away from central Moscow.

Despite its deterioration, a person can still circulate underground for hours beholding beautiful pieces of art and architecture. Each station reflects a particular theme of Russian history to admire and enjoy.

There were a couple of tricks to getting around on the Metro I had to learn since I wasn't familiar with reading Russian maps. I memorized the color-code for each Metro-line. Nearly every car has at least one color-coded map posted in a highly visible location. Different Metro cars have a different shade or color for the same line, however. On some maps it is difficult to distinguish between brown and orange, red and orange and the various shades of blue. There was also a difference between the older maps and the newer ones. As the colors faded, so did the Russian Metro maps.

Another way I would get around on the Metro was to memorize the number of stops the train was scheduled to make before it reached my destination. As the train approached each station, a broadcast was made over the public address system announcing the name of the approaching station and the following station or two. I learned to listen for words that sounded familiar. For instance, I knew that *Park Kultury* was the station where I switched trains to get home. *Oktyabraskaya* was the Metro for Church, etc. I was forced to concentrate, listening intently for familiar station names through muffled and distorted speakers. Using this method for a year, I only missed my station a couple of times.

The Metro station I frequented most was the *Kievskaya* Station. The entrance to the *Kievskaya* Metro was located right outside the *Kievski Vagzal* [Kiev Railroad Station], the connecting point for all travelers to and from the Ukraine and further south.

Our first journey took us to the outskirts of northeastern Moscow. Lena was the first one to teach us the ropes of maneuvering through the Metro.

At street level, the *Kievskaya* Metro entrance didn't look too inviting. We were taken back by the sea of gnarled and misshapen people reaching out with withered limbs and tugging at our clothing, but one man impacted us more than any other. He had no legs and no apparent waist, his body seemed to end just below his rib cage. Just looking at him, we wondered how he had managed to stay alive and endure the freezing Moscow winters. His hands were tightly wrapped in thick, soggy-looking wool socks used for padding as he heaved himself from station to station. He was sitting quietly on an odd shaped piece of splintered plywood in a corner he had claimed near the entrance to the station. Pinned on him was a well-worn, hand scrawled sign which informed the passersby that he was a Russian war veteran and in need of help. He had strategically placed a bowl for people to throw rubles into. Robin placed all the rubles she had folded up in her coat pocket in the dirty bowl.

There were numerous bands of men in their medium-length leather jackets huddled around each other attempting to stay warm in the frigid night air. Some were loud and boisterous, uttering words that meant nothing to us while others just silently watched the people pass them by, possibly looking for an opportunity to follow them into the tunnel and pick their pockets. One of my colleagues who traveled the Metro daily had forewarned me to not talk aloud or stare at anyone around a Metro entrance. "Walk with a purpose, ignore everyone around you and keep moving," was his advice.

The dimly lit street lights offered little assistance for those unfamiliar with the stairs leading down into the Metro tunnel. Black, sticky muck from the streets clung to our shoes like a thick glue. With no trash cans in sight, refuse was discarded wherever.

Making our way down the slippery stairs into the Metro was not the only challenge. The push and shove strategy from the airport also applied at the station. We either took part in all the pushing and shoving, or we became a victim with no one to come to our aid.

Most of the people who packed the Metro also carried, toted, and dragged boxes, suitcases, and bags loaded with goods, produce, and other finds. It was all we could do to avoid being knocked over by the rush of homeward-bound Russians.

During the last couple of months of our year-long stay, Yeltsin outlawed large, oversized boxes and luggage in the Metro because they had become a hazard. People had started moving entire flats via the Metro, furniture and all. There were so many goods being transported that there was little room left for people.

The mob of people we were following that day slowed as we edged closer to the glass window where we would purchase our Metro tokens. In fact, I noticed just up ahead that the crowd was at a stand still. As we were pushed forward by the throng of people behind us, I saw why.

Vendors were selling everything; books, beautiful bouquets of flowers -- although I couldn't figure out how they secured such fresh-looking flowers at that time of year -- cigarettes, vodka, candy bars and truckloads of pornography. Smut was peddled in all shapes and sizes, tabloid or magazine, front page or centerfold, male or female.

We finally squeezed our way through the crowd and stepped up to the tiny window. Lena purchased our tokens for the evening and quickly herded us toward the escalator leading down deep beneath the street.

The Metro was old and run down. The escalators had

seen better years, though the ones that were operating still ran extremely fast. Due to their speed, we were forced to get a running start as we climbed on, and again we experienced the bottleneck effect with everyone pushing and shoving. Many strategically used whatever they lugged behind them as a protective shield, warding off potential cutters.

Once on, the escalator carried us very quickly down into the belly of Moscow. It was literally breath-stealing to ride down so steep an incline at such high speeds, focusing on the point of departure several hundred feet below. We never did really get used to them.

Lena told us that the Metro had been built to double as a bomb shelter for the city in case of a nuclear attack. The entire Metro could be sealed off by huge thick steel doors. Later, I did see one brief documentary on the Metro, although I couldn't understand the language. It was old footage of people in white hospital gowns wearing white masks escorting mock crowds into the Metro while the steel doors closed behind them.

At the bottom of the escalator I could see a little glass booth with a large woman in an official-looking uniform watching the endless line of people pass her by. Her job was to slow down or speed up the escalator, based upon the need of the situation. However, it looked as if, from years of just sitting there doing virtually nothing, her senses to the world around her had become dulled.

I discovered that at the bottom of each of these escalators throughout the Metro sits a dulled, lifeless person, different in gender and size, but numb and unresponsive to the world around them.

We did, on one occasion, witness one of these corpses come to life. Suddenly and inexplicably she stepped out of her booth and began to rant and rave in verbal attack, only to settle down and drop back into her lifeless mode.

As we poured out into the hallways at the bottom, I was intrigued with the beautiful artwork on the walls, minus any graffiti. The floors were filthy, and there was a lot of trash, but there was no defacing of walls. Passengers didn't leave their mark with a marker or spray can, although some chose to leave their mark the natural way, by relieving themselves.

The architecture in the Metro was marvelous to behold, though we had little time to take it in. The speeding train screeched to a halt right in front of us. The bulging doors of the aging, dull green cars thrust open, releasing the pressure of people. Passengers were literally spewed out of the cars as the doors opened. I couldn't believe that so many could safely ride in one car. I soon learned that safety was not a primary concern in Moscow, thus the challenge to see how many people can be packed into one Metro car, trolley, bus, or jet.

We found ourselves being pushed right along with the crowd whether we wanted to be or not. It was tough keeping up with Lena, who had checked her courtesy at the Metro entrance. It was every man, woman and child for themselves.

There was no place to sit, so we latched on to the nearest rail and held on for a sixty mph ride. As we talked over the clatter of the tracks, I noticed everyone within earshot staring silently at us. Lena spoke loudly and openly with us. Feeling self-conscious, I asked her in a loud whisper if we should be talking in English while on the Metro.

"It is okay," she assured me. "Russians find Americans fascinating."

Sneaking quick glances around the car, I could see Russians gazing intently at our lips as we conversed. They seemed to watch our every word, perhaps longing to be able to understand, or perhaps understanding more than we assumed. Many Russians speak at least some English. I also noticed many of those sitting, both young and old, reading studiously as if cramming for a college exam.

Reading was still a favorite pastime for many Russians. A typical *Muscovite* is well versed in literature, they cherish their poets, philosophers, novelists and satirists. Many I spoke with often expounded upon pieces of literature as if they had been the original author or even the characters themselves within the pages.

At each stop, crowds would explode out of the doors with their belongings while others pressed in, allowing, if necessary, the door to close on them. When this happened, it was the signal for everyone to squeeze in a little tighter. Every time the train took off, its acceleration pushed everyone toward the back of the car. You really had to be sure of your handholds or you could find your nose buried in an unclean armpit. Having used the Metro only in a utilitarian manner to get from one place to another, I regretted not ever taking advantage of the numerous free offers to receive a guided tour of the Metro lead by a native *Muscovite*. I'm sure I would have found its history and legends fascinating. Sadly, I allowed my colleague's advice of "just keep quiet and keep moving" to be my guide instead.

7
MOTORISTS
MAYHEM
AND MEAT

"His name is Andrei. He is a very good driver and speaks very good English. He could also be your translator," Sergei said. "He was a mechanic in the Afghanistan war. He is a very safe driver and has a new imported car. You will not be sorry." Sergei, Customer Service Manger for our business center, was making every attempt to convince me that Andrei was the right person for the job.

Both Robin and I had decided that hiring a driver would be the most reliable form of transportation for our family. Though we did have other choices -- the Metro, trolleys, buses, trams, and taxis -- depending on them would involve adhering to set schedules and enormous crowds. I also didn't feel comfortable with Robin heading off into the city alone with a two-year-old on her hip and a five-year-old trailing behind. She didn't know the language well enough to ask for directions.

Anything could happen.

We had been told that we could get a full-time driver for one-hundred to one-hundred and fifty dollars per month, which included gas and upkeep of the car. Low though it may seem for an individual's monthly salary, the average Russian wage was twenty to twenty-five dollars per month, or the *ruble* equivalent. We would be willing to go substantially higher for the right person, as we considered it a wise investment.

"Okay, Sergei, please set up a time where I can meet with him," I said.

"I can have him meet you this afternoon on the second floor. You will not be sorry," Sergei assured me for the umpteenth time. "He has a wife and a daughter and doesn't drink or smoke. He is a good family man and needs a steady income."

I couldn't believe my ears. I assumed I'd have to settle for someone who didn't light up around the kids and would promise to pick us up only when sober. I didn't even consider his family life. Andrei was someone I looked forward to meeting.

Saturday afternoon arrived and I found myself shaking hands with a very nice looking, clean cut Russian of Polish descent. Andrei had an average build, but the way he carried himself made him appear much larger than he was. He wore a big smile that was easy to see even under his thick, dark moustache. His short, dark hair was clean and neatly combed. His mint green sweater looked new, perhaps purchased just for the interview. He looked just a couple of years younger than I.

We sat down and began to talk of common interests. His English really was quite good. I discovered he had a passion for music. Having been a musician in a number of local blues bands in Moscow, he talked of the local music scene and his two favorite groups, the Beatles and Deep Purple. He had an eight-year-old daughter, Julia, who was learning Spanish. He had been married ten years, a record for most *Muscovites*. He told me he drove some kind of Nissan. I discovered that major car manufacturers often gave the same car a different model name in Eastern Europe. Andrei's was the equivalent of a Nissan Sentra.

"Can you pick us up and take us to Church tomorrow morning?" I said. "This way it will give us a chance to ride in your car and observe how you drive." After seeing the way most Muscovites sped around the city, I was going to insist that Andrei exercise extreme care with my family in the car.

"No problem," Andrei responded excitedly.

"If it works out, we can sit down tomorrow afternoon and talk business," I assured him, sticking out my hand. "My family is very important to me. I must be assured that you're going to drive safely."

"I will do this," Andrei said with a tone of confidence and seriousness. "I will treat them like they are my own family."

Sunday morning arrived with a feeling of anticipation in the air. We were going to attend our first worship service in Moscow and simultaneously test drive our first driver candidate.

Andrei was early, a rarity for most Russians. He was waiting for us just inside the front door of the hotel. He had spent all morning carrying down buckets of clean water from his flat, washing his car inside and out from hood to trunk.

"This will be our last weekend here at the hotel," Robin said with a hint of regret in her voice, still thankful we had found a flat so quickly.

"If Andrei works out, we will have a way to get our bags to our flat next weekend," I said.

"Hi, Andrei. I would like you to meet Seth and Lindsay."

"Oh, so beautiful," he said with a big smile. "Okay, let's go," Andrei shouted with excitement.

I peered in Andrei's car with a look of surprise. The steering wheel was on the righthand side. It was a new experience for me, and a rather odd sight to most *Muscovites* also. Of the tens of thousands of Russian and foreign cars I saw in Moscow during my year's stay, only two or three had steering wheels on the righthand side.

As we climbed in, I asked if the seatbelts worked in

the back seat. He quickly jumped out, opened the back door, reached in and pulled them from deep within the seat. He brushed them off, and proceeded to buckle up the kids. "Yes, I have seatbelts, but in Moscow I never use them," Andrei said while offering a belt to Robin as well. "Okay, let's go."

He started the car and squealed the tires as he took off. He glanced over his shoulder and bolted out into a large intersection leading to the bridge going over the Moscow River. Andrei looked over and grinned every time I hit the floorboard with my feet out of habit and fear. Being on the wrong side of the car made it even more stressful. I always knew I was a white-knuckle flyer, and I began to think living in Moscow was going to make me a white-knuckle passenger.

Andrei was familiar with Lenin's Children's Library where the church service was to be held. He told me that he could get us there very quickly by taking several shortcuts through the city. His definition of quickly meant he was timing himself to see how fast he could get us there. All four of us held on, gripping anything within reach. I never knew a Nissan sedan could go so fast. After a few brief minutes we screeched to a halt in front of a large, square gray building.

"This is it," Andrei declared, jumping out of the car and opening the door for Robin and the kids.

"I think I'll take a few moments and speak with Andrei," I whispered to Robin. "Go on in and I'll catch up." Robin and the kids disappeared behind the large, dirty glass doors.

"How did I do?" Andrei looked at me, smiling with pride as if he had broken a world speed record.

"I need to talk with you," I said. "This is my family you would be responsible for. I love them. You would be taking my boy to *dietski sod* [kindergarten]. I don't know if I feel comfortable with you as our driver." Andrei's countenance fell. "I mean we like you personally, but if you were to become our driver, I would have to insist that you drive slowly."

Andrei's countenance rose again. "This is not a problem," he said. "I can drive slowly if you like. I just wanted you to be pleased with me."

"Driving slowly will please me."

After talking through some basic ground rules, we decided to go ahead and give it a try.

Thus began our relationship with a dear man who loved his Motherland with a passion. When asked if he could choose to live anywhere in the world, Andrei always said Moscow. In fact, probably 95 percent of all the Russians we met preferred their Moscow to any other place on Earth. Russians showed a deep sense of pride and tenacious loyalty when talking about their country.

Andrei not only became our driver, he became our translator, personal guide, and devoted friend. It did cost us many, many more *rubles* per month, but it was money well spent. Despite his stubbornness and bullheadedness at times, he was an answer to our prayers.

It was a miracle that Andrei only hit one pedestrian while he worked for us. Pedestrians are fair game on the streets of Moscow. In the States pedestrians have the right of way, in Moscow pedestrians are expected to get out of the way. You take your life into your own hands when you attempt to cross a street, any street, large or small, without a traffic light to slow cars down. The only warning a jaywalker will receive from an approaching car is a quick flash of the lights. If you're struck by a car, it's your fault. I witnessed an elderly woman hit by a car while attempting to cross the street in front of our flat. Unable to get to the other side of the road fast enough, the driver of the speeding car showed little mercy when he hit her. Moscow drivers have little compassion for pedestrians, feeling they are a nuisance in their way, and Andrei was no different.

Upon our return home one Saturday afternoon, having spent the day shopping at *Izmailovo,* Moscow's major outdoor flea market -- and sometimes Black Market -- Robin asked Andrei to stop by a little store near our flat so she could pick up some eggs. *Krupskaya* Street has a large boulevard engulfed in trees and flowers in the summer time. About halfway down the block is a large circular sidewalk lined with park benches filled with people. This gathering spot is right in front of the store. Approaching from the opposite direction, Andrei thought he could save a little time and gas by taking a shortcut across the boulevard via the sidewalk rather than going down to the end of the street to turn around. He received many scoffs and scowls from those forced to move baby carriages out of the way in order to make room for the car. After several near misses on the sidewalk, he maneuvered his way to the other side of the street. He pulled out into the street facing oncoming traffic and proceeded to pull up on the curb.

Robin darted into the tiny shop to buy the eggs while Andrei and I waited in the car. Several other drivers expressed their displeasure at what Andrei had done and how he was now parked facing the wrong direction. He just ignored them, preoccupied with his music.

Robin returned with the eggs in her little folding wire egg basket and slid in next to me. As we were getting ready to pull out, I noticed two businessmen carrying briefcases passing us by at a brisk pace. Without warning, both of them turned out into the street right in Andrei's path, not realizing that he was pulling out. As Andrei was looking over his shoulder -- I don't know why since he was facing the oncoming traffic -- he clipped one of them with his front bumper, knocking the man backwards. As Andrei passed him, uninterested in stopping to see if he was okay, the businessman stood back up and kicked the back panel of the car as it rolled by, brushed himself off and continued walking with his friend across the street as if nothing had happened.

Neither I nor Robin could believe what had just occurred. B ut no one touches Andrei's car without his permission. He slammed the car into neutral, hit the emergency brake and jumped out of the car, heading for the two men. I froze. I didn't know whether to follow him or stay put. After a few tense moments of shouting back and forth, Andrei walked back to the car, climbed in, jammed the car into gear and took off.

"What happened back there?" I said.

"I asked the man why he kicked my car," Andrei responded sounding vindicated.

"But you hit him."

"He should watch where he is going," Andrei said. "I told him that it was his fault for getting in my way. He agreed and apologized for kicking my car."

"And that's it?"

"Yes, there is no more problem. He agreed not to kick my car again."

We sensed a deep commitment in Andrei for our family's welfare while he worked for us. As friends, we often invited him up to have dinner with us after a long day's work, and each time heard his predictable response as he sat down to the table, "Do you always have different meals?" Accustomed to his daily ration of potatoes, bread and meat, he marveled at the idea you could vary your menu from evening to evening.

The Russian drivers' concept of punctuality was very

different from Americans. For instance, 9:00 a.m. can and often does mean 9:30 a.m. and noon means 12:30 p.m. After a couple of months of frustration, rather than simply giving in and living with it, I asked Andrei to begin picking me up thirty minutes earlier than pre-arranged. In order to get to work by 9:00 a.m., a twenty-five to thirty-minute drive from our flat, I told Andrei that he must arrive at 8:00 a.m. Thus he usually showed up around 8:25 a.m. I was less frustrated, and he felt like he was doing his job without fault.

Several months into the job I began to notice Andrei was arriving to work a little later each day seemingly dog tired. Sensing he might be getting ill, I asked if anything was wrong. He replied, "No, nothing is wrong," while rubbing his eyes. "I just stayed up last night purchasing *benzine* [gasoline]."

"What do you mean stayed up last night?"

"Every night when I take you home, I must buy *benzine* in order to come to work the next day."

"How long does this take you?"

"I arrive home about two-thirty or three in the morning," he said.

"What do you mean?"

"Waiting for *benzine* sometimes takes two or three hours. Then you can only purchase twenty-liters at a time. I must travel to different stations in the city to look for *benzine.*"

"You do this every night?" I said.

"Yes, until all of my gas cans are filled."

Now I understood why he always had five or six gas cans in his car at one time. I originally thought he was a little paranoid about running out of gas. But after learning of his difficulty getting fuel, I was able to recall the countless times I observed drivers, Andrei included, stop alongside of the road and add gas to their cars with the swiftness of a pit crew. Drivers were constantly pulling these twenty-liter gas cans out of their trunks and everyone behind them understood what had to be done. You had very few arguments on the road when inconvenienced, as everyone was in the same boat -- except, according to Andrei, the *Chechnya* mafia.

Many Russians believed the group called the *Chechnya* mafia to be the most ruthless crime group in all of Russia. From the way you heard a Russian speak about the *Chechens,* you would think that the whole country of *Chechnya* was mafia.

Andrei told me one time while waiting at a *benzine* station, he observed a little Russian man pulling up to the pump to take his turn at the twenty-liters, who was suddenly cut off by another car. Just as he was moving forward, a speeding BMW® swerved right in front of him, passing up the fifty or sixty cars behind him and stopping at the pump. Two thugs stepped out of the car. Andrei said that the little old man questioned the two young men, asking what they thought they were doing cutting him off. Their response was, "We are *Chechen.* We do what we like." At that, one of the bullies pulled out a large knife and proceeded to puncture the sidewalls of the little old man's four tires. They filled their tank, ignoring the twenty-liter allotment and then quickly sped away. The more often stories are told, the more they grow, nevertheless, the common Russian on the street will attest to the infamous tales of the so-called *Chechen* mafia.

Andrei wasn't the only driver we had. During our year long stay we had a total of three and three-fourths drivers. One driver lasted about forty-five minutes on his first day, so I'll give him a quarter. Another driver filled in for a few weeks for her dad, driving something that faintly resembled a car. I count her as the other half.

Andrei landed a job in Security at a local hotel, forcing us to begin searching for another driver. Though we truly hated to lose him, we were happy that he had found something a little safer and with a promising future off the streets of Moscow. Andrei assured us that we had no need to worry about finding a driver. He would personally find one for us that would be trustworthy and very careful, especially when the kids were in the car. In fact, Andrei had just the person for us. Volodya was his name. He was a good friend of Andrei's and had served in Afghanistan with him.

Volodya was a very quiet man, very unsure of his English, though very polite. His youthful sandy, curly hair, blue eyes and blond moustache made him look much younger than he was. He was also a smoker.

Seth, our five-year-old, seized every opportunity to warn Volodya of his impending death if he didn't stop smoking.

I think Volodya understood much more than he chose to express, which made it very convenient for him to often miss appointments. He and Andrei were 180 degree opposites. Andrei was outgoing, upbeat and happy, he did everything in the fast lane. Volodya was a true introvert, very melancholy, a true musician, and did everything in the slow lane. Whereas Andrei frightened us on the road with his speed, Volodya frightened us with his creeping along like a snail. Driving too fast, we feared Andrei would someday rear-end someone or something, whereas driving too slow, we feared someone else would rear-end Volodya. Volodya could easily turn a twenty minute ride into an hour long trip.

It became apparent after the first month Volodya had two things to overcome: tardiness and drinking. The latter would eventually get the best of him.

In order to get to work by 9:00 a.m., I insisted that Volodya arrive at my flat by 7:15 a.m. I really wanted him there at 7:45 a.m. but after several weeks, Volodya began arriving a little later each day. There were a number of days he didn't show at all, forcing me to catch a bus and the Metro at the last minute. Each time this happened, I demanded an explanation, and each time he used a popular Russian excuse; he had experienced a *catastroph*. He would then assure me that it would never happen again. I really didn't want to send the guy pack-

ing as I'm sure he needed the money, but he was beginning to force my hand.

Volodya seemed to enjoy the family and it was safer
than his previous job. Daily he scoured the streets as a
taxi driver, but using your own car as the taxi, you never
knew who or what might climb in. It was becoming
quite dangerous.

As Volodya started to feel more comfortable with us,
he started showing up every morning with alcohol on
his breath. I could endure tardiness, frustrating though
it might be, but I would not tolerate my children jumping into a car with a driver who was only partly there. I
gave Volodya several more chances to clean up his act. I
even asked Andrei to speak with him about the seriousness of the issue and the danger it imposed.

The final blow came on a Sunday morning. He had
been with us for a couple of months and had the opportunity to memorize our schedule. We usually spent
Saturdays at home, which gave him the day off. On
Sundays he picked us up for Church and brought us
home, thus freeing up his Sunday afternoons. Being
members of the Church's worship team -- a contemporary band that provided music for the service -- we had
to arrive early every Sunday for set-up and practice.
Each Sunday morning we would wait out in front of our
flat for Volodya to come creeping up the street. But this
day would be different.

While waiting for our ride, the kids chased pigeons
around in the snow. Pigeons in Moscow were really a

sign of the times. Nearly every bird had some type of deformity, half a beak missing, a nub where a toe or foot should have been, or a huge growth over one of its eyes. Some had nodules protruding from their heads. I often wondered what they had eaten or drank over the years to cause such a widespread deformity, and I remembered the *Chernobyl* disaster.

While I was looking up the street this particular Sunday, I kept hearing something crash behind me on the sidewalk near the kids. Every time I turned around I didn't see anything but the kids preoccupied with chasing the pigeons. Though we would have preferred to have Seth and Lindsay not chase the pigeons, it was tough to slow them down. We did educate the kids that they were never actually to touch them. After   the fourth or fifth time hearing the crash, Seth walked over to me closely examining a piece of frozen meat.

"Where did you get this?" I said.

"It's really neat, Daddy. It falls out of the sky and breaks into tiny pieces," Seth said.

"Show me where the rest of it is," I said.

Lindsay was still over in the corner of the building running in circles with the physically challenged birds. As I walked up I could see the whole area littered with small pieces of frozen meat. With a loud crash, another piece shattered right in front of us with enough force to knock someone unconscious.

"Get out of the way," I shouted, grabbing Lindsay and Seth.

I stepped back far enough to look up to see who was throwing the meat off the balcony. All I saw were two huge black crows perched on the edge of the ten story roof. On a balcony on the top floor, a Russian had laid out his winter's supply of meat. The crows, having discovered the stockpile, were picking at it. The meat was frozen solid and apparently too heavy to carry off, so the birds had started shoving the huge chunks off the edge of the balcony. As soon as we were gone, they planned on swooping down and carrying off the smaller, more manageable pieces.

As a Russian was coming out of the entrance, I shouted, pointing to all the shattered meat on the ground and then pointing up at the crows, attempting to visualize that they were carrying off someone's meat supply. She looked up, gasped and then quickly disappeared back into the entrance, apparently to warn the owner of the dwindling supply.

Some twenty minutes passed while we were busily engaged in frozen meat warfare and Volodya still had not showed up. I asked Robin to stay put and I would call Volodya's wife and see what had happened.

"*Ah-low*," the female voice answered groggily.

"Hello. This is Rick, Volodya's boss. Is Volodya there?"

"*Da*," came the reply. She put the phone down and began a conversation with someone obviously laying next to her.

A voice spoke, slurring every other word, "Hello.

Ah, Rick, this is Volodya."

"Volodya, we have been waiting outside for you. It is minus eight degrees. Why aren't you here? What has happened? What's the deal?" My questions revealed my frustration.

"Ah, Rick, I don't think I can drive you today," he said. "I had big party last night. Drank too much. I am still in bed."

"What?" I shouted. Volodya had crossed the line. "My family has been waiting out in the cold for over an hour. What are we supposed to do? It is too far to walk. We cannot take the Metro because I have all of this music equipment."

After a few moments of intense conversation with his wife, Volodya came back on the line. "Rick, I will come and take you to Church."

"Good, get here immediately." I hung up feeling more Russian than ever.

Remembering that Robin and kids were still outside, I grabbed a couple of extra scarves to keep warm. Getting ready to head out the door, the phone rang.

"*Ah-low,*" I said in an angry voice.

"Ah, Rick, this is Volodya."

"What do you want? You were supposed to be heading to your car right now."

"Ah, Rick, I do not think I can come to get you this morning. I cannot find my car and I do not think I could find your flat in all of Moscow. I am very sick from much drinking last night."

"Okay, you cannot find my flat today. I understand that. But tomorrow, you are not to find my flat again. And everyday from now on. You are fired." I think he was relieved to hear that so he could go back to sleep with a clear conscience.

The more I talked with Russians who spoke broken English, the more I began to speak in broken English myself. Fragmented sentences were becoming a way of communication.

I hurried back outside and told Robin what had happened. After venting a few minutes, we decided that we would make a mad dash for the Metro, guitars, music stands, music and all. We cinched up the kids and slid off to catch the bus that would take us to the Metro station. We arrived at the Church just before the service began. We never saw Volodya again.

We shared our frustration story with our friends at Church. A member offered us a ride back home and another volunteered to call one of their friends who knew of a driver in need of work. Desperate for just about anyone, I consented to let them make the contact. She told us that he was a fine Christian young man whose name was Peter. She was sure that he could pick me up the following morning for work and take Seth to school. We went home encouraged that our problem might be solved.

That afternoon our friend called us back and

informed us that Peter was available to start the next morning. We agreed on a price and laid out some basic rules. She told me that Peter spoke broken English -- that didn't that surprise me -- and looked forward to the opportunity to practice conversational English. Everything seemed to be working out better than expected.

The next morning the door bell rang. When asked who it was, a big booming voice shouted from the other side of the door, "It is PETER." I opened the door to an oversized teddy bear of a man with a big thick beard, rosy cheeks, and a broad smile.

"Hello, my name is Peter," he said as he stuck out his hand.

We briefly went through the introductions and then headed for the elevator. Robin and Lindsay had decided to tag along to ensure that Seth would get to school okay.

I'm sure we could have drawn a map and Seth would have eventually gotten to school, but if Peter needed to ask directions, our five-year-old would have been hard-pressed to tell him to turn right or left or continue straight. Once Seth learned how to say right, left, straight and stop in Russian, he often attempted to bark out orders from the back seat to the driver, any driver. *"Pryama* [straight]" *"Nyet, nyet, nalyeva* [no, no, turn left]" he would say, not having a clue where he was. This would often confuse a Russian taxi driver, especially since small Russian children rarely speak to adults, and send the taxi down a wrong street. We had to teach Seth to use these instructions only with our permission in order to avoid a serious accident resulting from a Russian taxi driver overreacting.

I had never seen a car like Peter's before. I can't describe the make or model, and neither could Peter. It looked as if he may have built it himself. What I did know was that it was very old, very tiny and very ugly, a mustard yellow with a shattered front windshield. The passenger seat had no back to it. Peter had to start the car from under the hood and then jump in, quite a challenge for such a large man with such a tiny car.

"This should be interesting," I whispered to Robin.

Robin and the kids climbed into the tiny back seat while I leaned forward in the front. It was more like sitting on a toilet seat with both arms resting on my knees than a car seat. Peter jumped in and backed over the curb with the car door still open. He took off, sliding around the corner, more preoccupied with his engine than his driving, as we sped off to work. We drove in silence, Peter engrossed in the sound of his car, and Robin and I exchanged *'who knows?'* glances at each other.

"Call me when you get back home," I told Robin, climbing off the seat. I shook hands with Peter, thanking him for his service. He smiled, though barely acknowledging me, still immersed in the strange sounds coming from under the hood. I blew everyone a big kiss, praying that we would be united in one piece later that evening. I confirmed with Peter what time he needed to pick me up from work, and I waved goodbye as they drove off.

Seth's school was located on the outer Ring Road, about forty-five minutes one way, which would mean Robin would be calling me about 11:00 a.m. At 10:30 a.m. the phone rang.

"Hi, hon, it's me," Robin said.

"Hey, you got back faster than I expected. How was it? Did Seth get to school?"

"Not good and no," Robin said. "The drive was not good and no, Seth did not get to school. It's been a bizarre morning."

They had only driven three or four miles down the road when *benzine* started gushing out of the engine and onto the street. Peter quickly pulled over to the side of the road, jumped out and inspected under the hood. He came back shaking his head and announced to Robin that she would have to find another way to get Seth to school and herself and Lindsay home. Robin became concerned, but Seth loved it. He loved the smell of benzine and it was always a treat for Seth to help our driver pour in his twenty-liter allotment.

"Maybe you call someone to come pick you up," Peter suggested.

"But I don't know the way home," she said fearfully. "I have no idea where we are."

"I cannot take you. My car is broken. It will take long time to repair it. I must call my brother-in-law," he explained. "I can call taxi for you too."

"No thank you. I do not know where we are," Robin shouted. "I need you to help us."

"I cannot. My car does not work. I must stay here," he responded. "I must tell your husband that I cannot work for him until my car is fixed."

After a few tense moments, Peter disappeared off down the street to make a phone call to his brother-in-law. When he returned he informed Robin that his brother-in-law would be taking her home, but he could not take Seth to school. "He speaks no English," Peter informed her. "I must stay with my car," he said repeatedly.

I hung up the phone disappointed that I was going to have to take the overcrowded trolley home again. I was going to be stuffed into a bus for an hour long ride with alcohol, boxes, and body odor.

Later that afternoon, Peter called the office and confirmed what Robin had told me. He assured me he was very sorry, but would not be able to be our driver until his car was repaired. He estimated it would take two or three weeks before it would be drivable again. I thanked him for the ride to work and hung up. I never found out what the problem was and I never saw Peter again.

"Rick?" Lydia, my secretary and translator, said. "Maybe I can help. I have a friend whose father needs some work. He has a very nice car and is an older gentleman. I'm sure he would be very safe."

"Yeah, Lydia, why don't you give him a call," I grumbled.

"I will have to call him when I get home tonight. Can I call you at home and let you know if he is able to work for you?"

"Sure. See if he can start tomorrow. That would be great," I said, knowing it probably wouldn't work out. *How I wished Andrei were back with us.*

The phone rang that night about 10:00 p.m. Robin and I had long since drowned our sorrows in home-made vegetable soup and had settled down to work a crossword puzzle.

"This is Lydia. I have some good news. Yevgeny would like to become your driver if you want him. I have told him the price and he has agreed to help you. He is willing to take Seth to school every day and take your wife shopping when she needs to go. He cannot take you to Church though. He goes to his *dacha* [country home] every weekend. It must be a very nice *dacha* since he goes there in the winter time."

"That's great," I said, relieved that we had found someone in such a short time. Drivers were becoming harder to find, they were demanding more money, and often refused to be the driver of just one client anymore. They could make a lot more money as a member of a local taxi mafia that claimed hotels throughout the city as their turf, as was the case for our hotel.

"He will be at your flat at eight a.m. tomorrow morning if that is okay with you," Lydia said.

"No problem. Robin will ride with us to make sure that he knows where Seth's school is." Robin rolled her eyes at me, expecting the worst, as I thanked Lydia and hung up the phone.

Yevgeny was a typical Russian man. He was difficult to pick out of a crowd because he blended so easily with everyone else. He was of average height with a round belly and sported a winter coat a couple of sizes too small. He had gray hair and gray eyes to match his gray *shapka* [winter hat]. He had big bushy eyebrows and long, gray nose hairs that made you want to run for a small pair of scissors. He had a pleasant smile revealing several gold fillings.

Yevgeny's car was by far the nicest and the cleanest of all of our drivers. It was a new *Lada* which he kept immaculate even throughout the messy winter. When other cars were filthy with road scum, Yevgeny managed to keep his car sparkling.

Looking back, I noticed that each of our drivers had peculiar driving habits. Yevgeny was no different. His driving was of average speed, but Yevgeny never looked where he was going. His mind always seemed to be drifting somewhere else. He often pulled out onto the street in heavy traffic not caring who was forced to slam on their brakes or swerve to miss him.

We were fortunate not to have gotten in the way of a

speeding mafia car. There were instances where thugs actually forced old men and women off the road, yanked them out of their cars, and beat them silly, just for getting in the way. Yevgeny was constantly in someone's way, and I often was tempted to scrunch down in the back seat and hide. Yevgeny didn't care, the road was his to own.

Everything went well for the first three weeks. Yevgeny was even on time, most of the time, he was faithful in taking Seth to school, and he was a big help to Robin with shopping. Yevgeny couldn't understand or speak a lick of English, but we were getting to know the Russian language more and more out of necessity and thus we were able to communicate in a few primitive phrases.

At the end of week three I received a phone call from Lydia. It seemed that Yevgeny had taken ill and would not be able to pick us up. He had asked Lydia to call us and see if it would be all right for his daughter to pick us up. He assured me that she was a good driver and that she knew Moscow well.

"He wanted you to know that his daughter used to be a very important driver. She was responsible for testing a car's performance on a special track," Lydia said.

"I guess we can do it temporarily. But I hope Yevgeny gets well and can come back to work very soon,"

"Wonderful. Olga will be there to pick you up in the morning. She will knock on your door."

The next morning, like clockwork, Olga knocked on the door. Once again we went through formal greetings. Robin would again tag along the first day to make sure that Seth got to the correct school on time.

We stepped outside and looked around for Yevgeny's car. We couldn't see it anywhere. Olga motioned for us to follow her around the corner to something I still hesitate to call a car. It was a very old and worn out Volkswagen Rabbit, blue, gray, white and rust colored and two of the windows had been shattered and replaced with irregular shaped pieces of plywood. Facing the front of the car, it looked as if the front end was ready to collapse over a pair of bald tires. The front seat on the passenger side did have a back to it, but it was broken and tilted back so far that you could barely see out of the windows, leaving no knee room for the passenger in the back seat. I didn't realize how much we had been spoiled by Yevgeny's *Lada.*

"Well, it's only for a few days," I assured Robin.

The car ground to a start with a huge cloud of blue smoke engulfing the interior, and didn't stop smoking until the engine was turned off. Olga was even slower than Volodya had been, not because she wanted it that way, but because the car was unable to travel any faster. It was a five speed which could only climb to third gear going down hill. Usually it struggled along in either first or second gear. Embarrassed pulling up to the hotel in that heap, I began having her drop me off at the gate. Seth needed the extra time to get to school anyway since his ride was now well over an hour long. Every day I would ask Lydia to call Yevgeny's wife and inquire about his condition, praying for a miracle.

Finally, Yevgeny did return to us for one week, but then came back down with a cold. His doctor at the *Poly Clinic* suggested he take another month off. I didn't know if we could tolerate his daughter's driving again, but we had no choice. I did ask if she could use his car instead, but the answer was an adamant "No." Yevgeny's *Lada* was his pride and joy and no one but Yevgeny was going to get behind the wheel.

We limped through a few more weeks of Olga's driving before Yevgeny finally returned, after which he stayed with us through the rest of our stay with few hitches.

One other feature of car ownership I noticed was the windshield wiper blade phenomenon. During the dry season or while their car is parked for any length of time, Russians remove their wiper blades. The stealing of wiper blades, or of cars themselves, is so pervasive that most Russians have a car alarm installed. It is common to walk into a parking lot and see all the wiper blades removed and little red lights flashing in every window seeking to deter would-be thieves.

At the first hint of rain or snow, all traffic stops while everyone gets out and reattaches their wiper blades. More than once I've seen it start to sprinkle while at a large intersection and without warning, everyone slams on their brakes, jumps out of their cars and installs their wiper blades. They then douse their windshield with an old liter Coke® bottle filled with water. A wiper reservoir cannot possibly hold all the water needed to keep the windshield clean from the muck thrown up by passing trucks and cars, so they keep an old one or two-liter Coke® bottle full of water for emergencies. In the winter, the reservoir under the hood stays frozen. They can't see through their windshield without the aid of a regular dousing at every intersection. Reattaching windshield wipers, dousing windows with water, and filling gas tanks have all become precision arts Russian drivers have perfected.

8
REPAIRS
RESTORATION
AND RINGWORM

"Hello. Who is it?"

Robin spoke loudly enough to be heard through the two doors. The doorbell had just rung, but it was 9:30 p.m. on a Monday night. We weren't expecting anyone, and there really wasn't anyone we knew in Moscow to expect.

"Rick, come here. There's someone on the other side trying to say something but I can't understand it." Robin spoke with a loud whisper trying to get my attention without getting theirs.

I laid my cards down, having been immersed in a game of Go Fish on the floor with the kids, jumped up and hurried to the door. We had heard all sorts of horror stories about ex-pats who were robbed by Russian thugs using a female voice as a decoy to get a door opened. We were the only American family in the area, and although everyone we had smiled at while moving in seemed friendly enough, we discovered that we had become the talk of the building, some good and some not so good.

We were the first Americans to ever live in that building. Old hard-line Communists didn't appreciate having an Imperialist family living near them. Young university students and married couples loved it because it gave them the opportunity to practice their English, and to observe how American families interact together. Riding in the elevator every morning and evening with Russians who lived in the building, I would always attempt to introduce myself in a friendly way. I quickly found out that our family needed no introduction. Everyone already knew who we were and where we lived, which I took both as a compliment and a warning.

"Who is it?" I said in a deep voice, preparing to somehow protect my family.

"Ummm, ummm, door, *pazhalusta* [please]," ordered a coarse female voice from the other side.

"Who is it?" I said again suspiciously. All I could hear was mumbling, and it sounded as if someone was with the woman. Suddenly, a door slammed and the voices stopped.

The telephone rang a few seconds later and Robin answered it.

"Ummm, ummm, opin zee door," stuttered the same female voice who had rung the doorbell.

"Who is this?" Robin said.

"Ummm, ummm, *eta* [this is] Vow-len-tee-na," she

said. "Open the door,"

The doorbell buzzed and someone was at the door again.

"Da. Who is it?" I said in my deepest businesslike voice.

"Vow-len-tee-na, ummm, Vow-len-tee-na," came the reply.

Unbolting our door was no small undertaking. Over the years our landlady had installed five locks and one chain on the inner door and two large bolts and another chain on the outer door. After going through the ritual of clicks and clangs, I swung open the heavy door to find an elderly, yet robust, woman standing in the hall with snow white hair carefully bunched up into a hairnet. She was smiling while peering through a bright turquoise colored toilet seat. It offered a strange image of a life size portrait encased in an oval blue picture frame.

Valentina walked into the flat as if she owned it. She saw the children on the floor in the living room playing a game and immediately ran over to them saying, *"Krasiva! Ochin krasiva. Kak krasiva.* [Beautiful! Very beautiful. How beautiful.]" She scooped Lindsay up and began smothering her in kisses. With a deep raspy tone of admiration and approval, she grabbed Seth and began saying, *"Kak balshoy,* [How big]" repeatedly. The kids loved the attention.

After a few minutes of hugging and kissing in the typical Russian *babushka* fashion, she got down to business. She again held up the toilet seat and headed for the restroom. "No problem," I said. "I can fix it." Apparently she didn't understand what I was saying for she began to walk me through how to replace the toilet seat, in Russian of course. I kept repeating, "No problem." Finally, after a few minutes of impasse, she began saying excitedly, "Muster, Muster, Muster. *Minutachku,* [Just a minute]." I looked to Robin for clarification and support, but she was just as dumfounded as I was. She wasn't ready to let go of the toilet seat, and she wasn't leaving. All I could say was, *"Ya nye panimayu* [I do not understand]." Then without any warning, Valentina exited our flat, with toilet seat in hand, and quickly disappeared into the elevator.

"What was that all about?" I said. "She has our toilet seat but she won't give it to us." Shaking our heads, we closed the door and headed for the living room.

A few seconds later the doorbell buzzed again.

"Who is it?" I said.

"Ummm, Valentina."

I opened the door and let her in. Following right behind her was an elderly man who looked to be in his mid-nineties. He was gaunt and very pale looking, as if he could drop in his tracks at any time.

Valentina attempted to introduce the frail gentleman to us. We shook hands and smiled at our new, white-haired friend. She was treating him as if he were a very important person. I saw why when the old man reached in his back pocket, pulled out a pair of old pliers and held them up with a smile revealing a mouth full of gold.

Valentina shooed Robin and myself out into the living room, though I would have preferred to change the toilet seat myself. I felt the old gentleman might strain himself too much, but he and Valentina actually seemed to enjoy being able to do something for their new neighbors. Robin and I moved into living room with the kids.

I could hear Valentina and the old man conferring back and forth. She was barking instructions while he was doing the work. We had just settled back down to our game of Go Fish when we heard a swoosh, followed by a river of water flowing into the living room. Alarmed, we both jumped up and ran for the bathroom. Valentina had grabbed the first thing she could get her hands on, our brand new plush, teal colored bath towels brought from America, and was sopping up water, using her feet to move the waterlogged towels around on the floor. For some unknown reason, the great-grandfather figure decided he should first remove the tank to get to the toilet seat, accidentally cracking the tank and causing the flood. He was barely able to reach back behind the toilet to turn off the water valve. All the old man could do was stare at me and make noises, "Oomph. Ummm. Oomph." Now embarrassed, he was speechless. He just glanced back and forth at both hands, the left one holding the pair of pliers and the right one holding a piece of broken porcelain. I began to fear the embarrassment might send him into cardiac arrest.

"What do we do now?" I said, knowing full well that they didn't understand a word. Valentina was busily wringing our soaked bath towels in the bathtub and then tossing them back onto the floor to collect more water. A fear of the unknown rose up inside me. What will we do for a toilet, I thought. I decided it was time to take action. I called Andrei, who was at the time still my driver, hoping he would be home so he could translate for us. We were in luck.

"Valentina told me that the Master will be at your flat tomorrow morning. He will fix your toilet for you," Andrei informed me.

"What are we supposed to do until then?"

"It is not a problem," Andrei said. "Just use a large pail of water to wash everything down." The toilet, being a European style toilet with a ledge and no bowl, was going to take a tremendous force of water to move anything along. I prayed for a miracle of constipation for the next twelve hours.

I heard a banging as someone was knocking very loudly at the door. I asked Andrei to hold on, set the phone down, and headed for the door. Valentina had already taken it upon herself to answer it for us. It was a middle-aged woman with a scowl on her face. I thought for a moment she and Valentina were going to go to blows. After a few tense moments of shouting back and forth, the woman stomped off. Valentina jumped on the phone and quickly informed Andrei of what was going on and then handed the phone back to me.

"This woman who lives below you thinks you are trying to drown her with all this water. It is coming into her bathroom. She wanted American dollars to make everything right. Valentina told her that she would get no money and that is the end of it." I thanked Andrei and hung up the phone.

The little old man, now seated, was visibly shaken from the whole ordeal. I told him as best I could that there was no problem. *"Da zaftra,* [Until tomorrow]" I kept repeating. Valentina and the gentleman said their goodbyes and departed for the night, with toilet seat in hand. Maybe she thought I would only compound their disaster if she left it with me, though most likely she merely wanted to see her project through to the end.

The Master Plumber did arrive the next morning as promised. The reason I knew he was the real Master Plumber was because he had two pairs of pliers in his pocket. Valentina was there with the toilet seat in hand ready to hand it over at just the right moment. Everything went off without a hitch. After sitting for weeks on a toilet seat wrapped in black electrical tape long since turned sticky, I couldn't wait to try our new one out.

We had been told that we were very fortunate to have our flat; it was large, relatively speaking, and very secure. Though Yelena left behind in the bookcases and cabinets much of the stuff that she had previously agreed to take with her, it was a comfortable situation to be in.

When we first arrived, Yelena was very excited about what she had done to the flat on our behalf. She had purchased children's blankets for the kid's beds with airplanes and dolls on them. She had bartered for a large box of light bulbs, though not one of them fit in any of the sockets. Three boxes of fuses were purchased for electricity failures, which occurred at least two or three times a month. She had agreed to pay our electric and phone bill, about three or four dollars per month combined. But perhaps the most memorable thing Yelena did for us was to decorate our bedroom.

Yelena told Lena, our flat finder, that when she saw Robin and me for the first time, she knew we were in love. Our new landlady had it in her mind from day one to create a bedroom that would provide a sensual environment to "enhance our love." Being a single mother herself, perhaps she longed for someone to do the same thing for her someday when she remarried. The resulting bedroom was a sight to behold. Everything had been decorated in red satin. The curtains, red with large paisley patterns, reached the floor and beyond. The bed was made up of an undersized twin bed with a tiny cot pushed up next to it, covered with rolled up blankets to bring it up to the approximate level as the other, and then more rolled up blankets between the two to provide a smoother surface. A red satin bedspread was placed very neatly over the makeshift bed to make it look larger than it was. She accented the bedspread with small red satin pillows. To add to the ambience of it all, she had purchased six tiny lamp shades covered in red moire for the mini-chandelier so when you walked into the room all you saw was red. She couldn't wait to show off her interior decoration skills and while we smiled in appreciation for all her efforts, we frowned when we rolled back the bedspread later that night.

The first item on our action plan when we moved in was the water. More often than not, we found ourselves bathing in water reflecting a slight oil film on the surface. Washing your clothes in it was acceptable, bathing and washing your hair in it was tolerable, but drinking it was our greatest concern. It startled us to see Andrei, our driver, come in from a long day of shopping and down two or three glasses of the undiluted stuff without a thought.

Robin had found a water filter well-known in the States at one of the joint-venture grocery stores, but we were more concerned with disease and parasites so common in that part of the world. Then a friend told us about a water filter we could purchase at a particular *Poly Clinic*. The filter was specifically developed for the victims of *Chernobyl*. The price of five dollars was a little too good to be true, but it had documentation Andrei read to us confidently assuring its effectiveness. It even claimed that it could reduce radiation levels, and kill and remove everything that ran through it.

Robin took a chance and bought the filter. We used the little red canister throughout our stay, praying that nothing would get through the filter that could do us bodily harm. Inconvenienced -- the definition of life in Russia -- we were forced to wait seemingly forever to fill a glass. We had to let it trickle through the multiple layers of what looked like tiny BB's in the filter. I thought at times we might die of thirst just waiting for the water. Robin would then run the end product through the filter purchased at the joint-venture store for taste. It soon became routine to prepare a gallon of drinking water in advance to avoid the waiting. It was just one more thing to add to our ever increasing daily routine.

As summer rolled around, we found ourselves faced with several new challenges. The first challenge was corralling the kids every night and convincing them it was nighttime although still broad daylight outside. The darkness didn't penetrate the sky until 10:30 or 11:00 p.m. in June and July, and sending the kids to bed at 8:30 seemed like torture. Then we discovered the positive side; in December the kids started yawning around 5:00 p.m. and by 6:00 p.m. they were begging to go to bed, allowing Robin and myself more time to be alone together on those long winter nights in our ever-shrinking flat.

The second challenge was to successfully fend off the Metro Mosquitoes. We knew we were in for a battle when we read an article in one of the local newspapers that described in detail the tenacity of those irritating blood suckers. The Metro Mosquitoes in Moscow were the meanest, thirstiest, and most resilient mosquitoes I have ever encountered. They had become immune to most insecticides and were virtually indestructible. They were also vicious, sometimes biting us six or seven times in one night. I inherited a natural deficiency of vitamin B-1, or so I was told, which meant that a biting insect of any kind within blocks will track me down. The kids inherited the same deficiency, and while I could take the vitamin B-1 straight, the kids were too young to take any supplements beyond their daily children's chewable vitamin, which was not enough protection against the Metro Mosquitoes.

I recall Lindsay waking up several days in a row with her hands, arms, and legs red and swollen from a hungry predator. Because we had never seen a reaction to bites so severe, we thought it might be a strange Russian disease, and Yelena added to our fears with the medical books she left behind. There were graphic illustrations of things that attacked the human body in ways we could never imagine, all there for our reading pleasure right in our own living room. Not being able to read any of the accompanying descriptions compounded our escalating fears. We finally found the culprit, a lone mosquito on the ceiling in the corner of the bedroom. Robin eventually had netting sent over which allowed us to leave the windows open at night. Moscow was warm and muggy during the summer nights, and the air inside the flat became stifling without a flow of fresh air from the outside.

The third challenge was the citywide restoration period. I called it the "Restoration Blues." The Moscow water department was centralized, a carry-over from Communism. Even the hot water system was centralized which meant there were no hot water tanks in the flats. All the hot water came from regional heating stations throughout the city. When it was operational, we never ran out of hot water and never had to pay water bills. The downside was that when summertime rolled around, we knew that the restoration period would come unannounced as a thief in the night.

Every summer each heating station shut off the hot water in their region for a period of one month, give or take a couple of weeks. Each year we had no hot water in our flat for full thirty days. The city shut off the water without warning and there was no one to call to get an idea when it would return. Andrei, our driver, lost his hot water June fifteenth and did not get it back until late September. I would regularly ask how he and his family were managing, and suggested that he call his local City Council member to see if he could get some assistance. Two months without hot water seemed a little too long. Andrei just laughed and said, "A Russian learns to live without such things. We are forced to make do with no answers. It is as it is."

We were more fortunate. Our hot water was shut off

for exactly thirty days. The first day we turned on the faucet and found nothing, we scrambled to purchase four oversized pots for boiling water. We noticed that most of the large pots readily available at the local markets mysteriously disappeared during the summer months. Our daily ritual of bathing took an extra hour and a half. Doing dishes and washing clothes added another couple of hours. The entire day was spent filling pots, boiling water, and emptying pots. It seemed to never end. It was amazing to see how much we had come to rely on hot water for our daily routines. We just assumed hot water would always be there. When the hot water did return, we prayed and thanked God. Even the oil slick on the surface of the bath water didn't look so bad.

It seemed that as each month passed in our flat we were faced with a new challenge or difficulty to work through, but nothing could have prepared us for the catastrophic events we experienced with the landlady herself. Five months into our lease, Yelena began to see American dollar signs. Russians had not advanced to our Western level of materialism. They were still in the early stages of greed. Convinced that she could rent her flat for hundreds of dollars more per month to someone else, Yelena attempted to evict us numerous times. She regularly showed up, often unannounced, with documents in hand expecting to expel us. She screamed at us, threatened us and tormented us weekly for months, but we had nowhere else to go. Forced to mediate between Yelena and our family, Lena, our flat finder, and Andrei, our driver, concluded that she was the craziest Russian woman they had ever met.

Yelena claimed we stole her Czechoslovakian crystal, although it was on the shelves in plain sight, and she wanted dollars; she claimed we soiled her Persian rug, although it was on the wall, and she wanted dollars; we replaced her two things she called beds with two brand new twin beds, and she wanted dollars; our faucet leaked, and she wanted dollars; we put up mosquito netting for her windows, and she wanted dollars; we stored her books in the back of the kid's bedroom to make room for our things, and she wanted dollars.

We will probably never realize all of the effects our flat had on us. The winter nights were stifling from the constantly radiating heating pipes with no thermostat to adjust. That, too, was centralized. We had a leaking Russian-made microwave we purchased from a local appliance store. Our Russian-made freezer had a disclaimer against death in case of an explosion. We had lead paint and lead pipes. Skinless, boneless chicken breasts were brought to us each week by our little *babushka*. She refused to tell us where she purchased the poultry, but it was the meatiest and tastiest chicken we had ever eaten, however we were hesitant to turn off the lights for fear the chicken might give off a greenish glow in the dark. Our non-refrigerated, long-life milk, we succumbed to buying for convenience sake, sat for an undeterminable amount of time in a warehouse somewhere in Moscow. There was a unique quality to our fruits and vegetables, fertilized eggs, *shashleek* [Russian pork shish kabob cooked over an open fire], and virtually everything we bought there.

Nine months into our twelve-month stay, Seth, our five-year-old, contracted a particularly resistant strain of ringworm. Robin was convinced that the regular bathing in the affected water had something to do with it, or at least seemed to irritate it.

Seth had over one hundred and fifty ringworm sores on his little body. I had originally thought that the first tiny sore on his tummy was a rug burn. We often wrestled on the floor, which was covered with something softer than concrete but rougher than AstroTurf. I applied some salve to the sore and covered it with a bandage. The next morning it had doubled in size and like two mice left to themselves overnight, it began to multiply. It eventually spread to every crack and crevice on his entire body. In desperation, we went to the American Medical Center, known for its exorbitant fees and selective assistance, and picked up some serious topical ointment. The cream sent it dormant, but didn't clear it up. We finally had to have a powerful prescription express-mailed to us.

We were assured that the medicine would completely eradicate the internal fungus. Seth was given a prescription of fifty pills. Our doctor back in America told
us that it would take all fifty, taken once a day, to cure
the ringworm. The prescription ran out one week before
we were scheduled to return to the States, and much to
our disappointment, the very day after Seth stopped taking the drug, the ringworm began to return. Oddly
enough, when we stepped off the jet in New York City,
the once again active ringworm cleared up and never
returned.

9
SHOPPING
SWAPPING
AND SWIPING

Shopping in Moscow was by far our greatest lesson in frustration. Even with driver, it was still a major undertaking for Robin three full days a week. That was if we chose to try eating healthfully. If all we wanted was a hearty meal, we merely had to step out to the corner of *Krupskaya* and *Vernadskova* and congregate behind the dumptruck load of potatoes. Men would stand in the back of the truck and toss sacks out to the crowd. You took what you got, there was no renegotiating with the local farmers. The potatoes were cheap, but they didn't provide much variety.

Robin's first adventure each day was to exchange dollars for *rubles*. Since the *ruble* fluctuated hourly, it was unwise to stock up. Every morning she watched the local 2x2 network on the black and white Russian TV and listen for the daily exchange rate. She couldn't understand the rest of the financial report, but she did understand *rubles,* and she quickly became a pro at the numbers out of necessity.

Once Robin found out the Central Bank's exchange rate, she would have our driver take her to one of several local exchange commissaries that were known to have good rates. She was always able to get a better rate than the rate announced on TV, she only used the morning report as her starting point. Sometimes, without notice, small trailers would appear on sidewalks with a little sign posted on the door that they were open for business. These traveling "ATM machines" offered good exchange rates if you could ward off the fear of being surrounded by automatic weapons while handing over your dollars. Once they knew you wanted to exchange dollars for *rubles,* you were escorted inside the trailer, one at a time, while two or three men stood over you with machine guns ready. After only a few intimidating visits, Robin became immune to the sight and was able to immediately get down to business.

On her shopping days Robin traveled one of three directions. One day she would hike the State-run store route. Another day she would take the *rynak* market route. Still another day she would follow the hard-currency route. These decisions were based upon her never ending network of shoppers who would let her know what was available and where, what was or wasn't in the cupboards at the time, and who was coming to dinner.

Robin seemed to enjoy the *rynak* market route the

most, though it was probably the most dangerous. A *rynak* is a farmer's market, some were outdoors, some were indoors. A few were stocked with local produce, but most had the southern produce carried by Georgian peddlers. Some were small, some filled large buildings like county fairgrounds. And all of them, transient in nature, were compelling to Robin's adventurous side.

Gypsies would often frequent the entrances looking for gullible targets. A colleague of mine had invested in several thousand one-inch-thick dowel rods. After trying to figure out what to do with them for several days, we decided that they would make an excellent "Gypsy Stick." Cut to the right length, they just might do the trick when attempting to fend off gypsy women, children and teenagers intent on mugging you. I brought home an eighteen-inch "Gypsy Stick" for Robin's protection. Being an artist at heart, she painted it with psychedelic patterns, using bright colors that would definitely get someone's attention. We drilled a hole through one end for a leather strap so she could throw it over her shoulder for easy carrying. It became her daily companion for the rest of the year, and it must have worked its magic. Not a single gypsy approached her, even for a handout, but they all seemed to notice the stick. I didn't think they could read the English words, "Gypsy Stick" painted on it, but maybe I was wrong.

The *rynak* market offered the most wonderful fruits and vegetables one would care to see, though they were quite expensive. Our local *rynak* was sheltered by a large round roof which protected people from the elements but not from the insects. Georgian men usually ran the stands, barking at each shopper as they passed, tempting them with the luscious fruit. It was fun to watch Robin at work. With her long blonde hair, the dark-haired Georgians couldn't help but notice her. As she made her rounds from booth to booth, she received proposals, propositions, and invitations of all sorts. One peddler at our local *rynak* made the effort to speak with her every week, and it soon became a serious ploy to win her for his own. She showed him her wedding ring, she refused his advances, she learned the phrase "just friends" in Russian and used it repeatedly, but try as she might, she couldn't dissuade the would-be Georgian husband. She had become the love of his life and he wanted everyone to know it. It wasn't until his advances turned from pertinacious to petulant that Robin became concerned. Becoming ever more fluent in conversational Russian, Robin finally stopped him in his tracks with one terse and animated phrase, *"Minya moozh, balshoy* [My husband is very big]." She warned him with a full sweep of her arms in a manner far removed from her usual good-natured banter with the man. He immediately ceased, although he did give her a very expensive bag of cashews, Robin's favorite, as a sort of final token of his affections. He never flirted with her again.

Robin quickly learned their game. If she saw something she liked, usually the fruit or vegetable the

Georgian was holding up as a lure, she would begin to bargain. Once the price was agreed upon, the salesman quickly exchanged the showpiece for a less attractive piece and nonchalantly shoved it into a bag and handed it over. They were very quick at the exchange, but Robin caught them every time and would pull the substandard fruit or vegetable out of the bag and demand the one he was originally offering. The seller would apply the guilt pressure by telling her that she would be taking away his only showpiece, leaving him with nothing left to display. I think the salesmen both enjoyed and regretted Robin catching them, for they always ended up exchanging the good stuff back with a sardonic smile.

The local hard-currency stores, otherwise known as joint-venture stores, provided a small taste of home for an exorbitant price. If you were willing to pay for it, in inflated dollars or marks, you could have just about anything you wanted. The only obstacle was that the joint-venture stores were never very close to one another. Our driver knew that he was in for a long hard day of driving if it was hard-currency day. There were days when Robin would have to hit seven or eight stores in opposite directions throughout the city. She did this when she wanted canned goods with readable labels, long life milk, cheese, mixes, toiletries, etc. After several months of trial and error, she learned which stores would normally carry what, and at what time of the month. It shortened her eight-hour day into a five or six-hour day. She learned early to buy what she saw then and there. If she hesitated, someone else would buy it.

One odd aspect of shopping in a hard-currency store was their method of giving change. They rarely had any silver coins, so instead, they offered candy. You could purchase something for four dollars and twenty-five cents, give them a five-dollar bill and they would stick a bowl of candy in your face, expecting you to accept the edible currency in lieu of the seventy-five cents. The candy was probably worth five cents, but you were expected to only take one or two pieces.

Before we left, Yeltsin had ordered the hard-currency stores to change over to *rubles* only. The dollar was outlawed on the streets of Moscow, in a futile attempt to boost the Russian currency and economy. Few stores that we frequented ever fully made the changeover, and the dollar never disappeared on the street. If you held up dollars in a joint-venture store and said, "No *rubles*," they would gladly accept it and shove it into their already overstuffed cash registers.

The easiest yet most frustrating day of the week was the State-run store day. To save money and to have a real taste of Russian futility, Robin decided that there were certain things she could purchase at these shops, often located on the first floor of an apartment building. The shops were often close by and within easy reach, but once she entered the State-run store, she encountered the full force of Russian red tape.

Normally, each shop specialized in a particular food group. Simple pictures were painted on the display windows of each store for quick reference or for those who didn't read Russian. There was a shop for *khlyep* [bread], a shop for *malako* [milk] and *syr* [cheese] products, a shop for *ptitsa* [poultry], a shop for *ryba* [fish], a shop for *frukty* [fruits] and *ovashi* [vegetables], and a shop for *myasa* [meat]. When she could stomach the filth and often putrid odor, she could sometimes find a steal in these holes in the wall. She could also journey to the *gastranom* [a Russian style supermarket], nothing like the Western definition of a supermarket, and stand in the queue.

Russians in State-run stores have one way and one way only of doing things, the way it's always been done. When you walk in a State-run store the first thing you see is a counter. Everything is usually located behind the counter. There is very little within reach for you to inspect without first asking for permission. You must work your way into the impatient crowd, the queue, by rocking back and forth against elbows, bags, boxes and purses until you finally reach the counter. Once at the counter, you must make every attempt to get the clerk's attention and let them know you're interested in examining something. Russian employees seem to make it their job to ignore you until they're forced to do otherwise. You must begin speaking loudly, making a spectacle of yourself if you're a foreigner, while pointing to the item you wish to view. Finally, if you are persistent, they will hand you the item. You then inspect it while the employee watches. They will demand a decision to be made immediately.

Once a decision is made to purchase the food or goods, you must hand it back to the employee and shake your head yes or no. Then you must make your way back out of the crowd and proceed over to the *kasa* [cashier] and describe what you want to buy. If you encountered a relatively helpful employee at the counter, they might have handed you a bill stating what it was you were intending to purchase. You then paid the *kasa* the proper amount of rubles.

Once the *kasa* was paid, you marched back over to the queue you just left and began once again to make your way to the counter. Often the clerk will have forwarded your item to another person a few more feet down the counter, but you're never sure so you still have to check. She may have moved it to another area specifically designated for pickup. If that was the case, you had to present your proof of payment to the original clerk so they could record it in their ledger and then proceed to the pickup point. Only when they fully inspected your bill were you handed your purchase. All that for a kilo of flour and a dozen eggs.

If you had your walking shoes on, the *kiosk* was

another world of shopping. Where you lived determined whether or not it was feasible. The large conglomerate of *kiosks* were normally found at busy intersections and around Metro stations. The *kiosk* was a great place for a Russian to become self-employed. They could set their own hours and decide what was going to be sold in their little business. The only draw back was the various mafia groups demanding protection money for the small businessman to stay in business.

Robin happened upon an incident one morning that made the danger of doing business in Russia clear to us. She had just dropped Seth off at the school bus stop and was going to grab a few things in the small makeshift market area near *Lomonosovsky* and *Vernadskova*. She and Lindsay were preoccupied, minding their own business, as they turned a corner and came face to face with two thugs roughing up a local *kiosk* owner. The bloodied man, already beaten senseless, leaned against the *kiosk* while each bully continued to take turns punching him. Each would ask him a question. He would respond quietly and submissively. In turn, they responded with a loud *"Nyet,"* and hit him again in the face. Others walked by, oblivious to the beating, as if nothing out of the ordinary was happening. There were no *Militsiya* or *GAI* [traffic policeman] to be found. Completely helpless physically, she could only turn away and offer a prayer for the man.

Crime in Moscow touched everyone at some point. I remember coming home from work one day and finding Robin had not yet returned from shopping. There were no notes so I didn't know which direction she had gone. Since it was so late in the day, I guessed she had gone the hard-currency route. I had just changed my clothes when Andrei, my driver, walked through the door with Robin trailing behind. She was sobbing uncontrollably and my heart became gripped with fear.

"I'm sorry, Rick. I'm so sorry." Both Robin and Andrei spoke simultaneously.

"It's my fault," Robin continued. "I shouldn't have done it."

"What?" I trembled. "What are you talking about?"

"Your shirts."

"What about my shirts?" I said. "And where are the kids?"

"They're with the sitter outside on the playground. You didn't see them?"

"No, but I wasn't looking for them. What about the shirts?"

"Andrei and I went to *Novy Arbat* Street to pick up some things at the Irish House (a hard-currency store). On the way, I stopped by the hotel to pick up your dry-cleaning as a surprise for you. Since it was getting warmer I thought I might go ahead and get all your short-sleeve shirts ready. Anyway, Andrei parked in what seemed to be a safe place, out in broad daylight. We put the dry-cleaning bags in the floorboard of the back seat and locked the car. We were only in the store for ten minutes. When we returned, everything was gone. Andrei's passport and legal documents he has to have in order to drive in Moscow, and all of your shirts. All twenty of them. I'm so sorry," she wept bitterly, "you don't have a single short-sleeve shirt left."

I did have some interesting short-sleeve shirts, but I assured Robin that having them stolen was the least of my worries. At least they didn't physically harm her.

We were able to find two or three shirts in Moscow to replace the ones I lost and my sister-in-law found a way to get a couple more to me via a traveler coming our way. I spent many an hour with Andrei cruising *Novy Arbat* Street looking for anyone wearing one of my shirts, though I don't know what I would have done if I had seen someone wearing one. I never saw a single shirt and we chalked it up to experience.

Purchases couldn't be put in the trunk because Russians carry two or three twenty-liter gas cans at all times. Storing these cans for years in their trunk causes it to take on the odor of a mechanic's garage.

We learned our lesson about putting things in the trunk when we sent our driver to McDonalds one night for our dinner. Moscow has the world's busiest McDonalds and with the rise of entreprenuerialism in Moscow, you don't have to get out of your car anymore. Young teenagers will run up to you and ask if they can purchase your food, for a fee of course, while you wait in the confines of your car.

That particular night we surprised the kids with the announcement that burgers and fries with shakes were going to be arriving soon. It was a rare treat, and Seth and Lindsay were ecstatic. When our driver delivered our food, I noticed the distinct odor of gasoline. I asked him if he had experienced car trouble. "No," he said, though he did have to run another errand and decided to put our food in the trunk of his car for safe keeping.

The food was cold and pungent, so I placed the burgers and fries, still in their packaging, spotted with grease and gasoline, in the microwave to heat them up, thinking somehow that the returning heat might return the original flavor too. I didn't consider that the place could have gone up in flames mixing those cold, lethal burgers with heat and energy.

We did eat the tainted burgers and fries, but the heat didn't take away the noxious fumes. We sat down to dinner and made the best of an otherwise disappointing event. We had become more Russian than we realized; I belched gasoline fumes for days.

10
FOOD
FIZZ
AND FIESTAS

When shopping for anything in Moscow, if we saw something we thought we might need then or anytime in the future, we purchased it right then, because chances were very good that the person worming his way in behind us had every intention of buying it if given the opportunity. They practice impulse buying in its purest form, seeing and buying things simultaneously. It is a skill the wise in Moscow hone quickly.

Robin had several great finds during her escapades through the hard-currency stores. Before we went overseas, we heard stories of entire families gathering around an orange or two, or perhaps a cluster of grapes and relishing the moment of victory. They would carefully divide up the spoils between each family member and partake together around the tiny kitchen table. I couldn't comprehend such a moment, but then again, I had never lived in a foreign country. I was used to the multitude of foods and beverages as close as the local convenience store. Such an ordeal over a single orange was unthinkable.

Experience has been a great teacher. There were times when we would find something special and share it deliberately with each other. I didn't know a good peach could bring such ecstasy, but it did. Actually, fresh produce -- some of the best we have ever eaten -- had become readily available by the time we took up residence in Moscow, but as with any good thing there, it came at a high cost, one that average Russians could rarely afford.

Peddlers from the Southern regions were to be found on every street corner and in every *rynak* [market] with fruits and vegetables that would shame most American grocery stores. The only disadvantage was that fresh produce was truly seasonal there as opposed to our nearly year-round supply in the States. We learned to savor the warm season of bounty and stock up on canned goods from the hard-currency stores for the leaner, cold months.

There were a couple of things we did run across, however, that proved to be more precious than gold. Robin's shopping sprees often took her to *Lux*, a hard-currency store built for the 1980 Olympics, near our flat. They called the area Olympic Village. We could never figure out the *Lux's* buying/stocking calendar, so we shopped the place weekly and purchased based on the principle that what we saw today may not be available the next day, or any time in the future. Most of the store contained imported sweets, with three to four aisles devoted to every imaginable cookie, candy or cake, but on one particular day they had just stocked the shelves with things we thought we would never see in Russia. Right before Robin's disbelieving eyes was enchilada sauce, refried beans, and taco and tostada shells. Without giving it a second thought, Robin snatched up all of the Mexican food she could fit in her basket and headed for the cash register.

On her way to the checkout stand she noticed another nugget of gold. It was yellow, it was in block form, and it was expensive: cheddar cheese. We had lived on various forms of inexpensive and sometimes questionable Russian cheese for a good number of months, as well as enjoying the relatively new importation of Gouda and Edam cheeses. We later discovered a Russian cheese in the family of Mozzarella or Monterey Jack that was delicious and made a fine pizza topping, but it was about ten times the cost of other Russian cheeses. Still, they had nothing that remotely compared to cheddar, a must in a Mexican dish. Once we took possession, we began making plans for our first fiesta.

A couple of weeks later, Robin was on another adventure which led to the Mother Lode. A small, relatively inexpensive hard-currency store called the Virginia House, known especially for its uniquely

American junk food, had just set up a large display of tortilla chips. Corn in Russia is mistakenly reserved for livestock feed and its more glorious uses were as yet a mystery to most Russians. It must have been for this reason that Robin came upon them untouched. Robin bought all twenty-four sixteen-ounce bags. Not only did we buy enough for us for the next four months, but we purchased the rest as gifts for friends. Our popularity increased tenfold.

Another find in the same store proved even more delightful to us: Dr. Pepper®. Being a Pepper family, we were dismayed to discover the Russians had yet to become a Pepper too. Andrei, our driver, probably thought Robin was crazy to buy such strange things. We offered him a taste of the foreign brew, but he just wrinkled up his nose and handed it back to us. Russians seemed to prefer Coke®, Pepsi®, and Fanta®.

I remember when one of the big two soft drink companies built a bottling plant in one of the southern countries in order to provide healthy competition as well as boost the economy. The other soft drink company already had a stronghold in that region and had become the standard for all. With a noble attempt to honor the new investment, the President of the country held a press conference. During that conference and with a smile on his face, he took a sip and held up the new soft drink and proclaimed, "It tastes just like . . ." *the other soft drink giant.*

We stored the cases of Dr. Pepper and doled out one a week. Going without for eight months taught us to conserve to make it last. We even gave one six-pack to an American who had been out of the States for well over a year. When we discovered that Dr. Pepper was his favorite drink, we couldn't resist the temptation. We carefully wrapped it up and gave it to him as a birthday present. He nearly cried when he opened it.

Another big find was salsa, both hot and mild. Another hard-currency store, Farin & Swanson, had imported some off-brand that wasn't half bad. I think it was manufactured in the Netherlands. Once again, Russians left it alone because they didn't know what to do with it, and again, Robin bought the entire case for family and friends. We gained the ability to hold a number of "South of the Border" fiestas for our American guests and looked forward to the opportunity to expose Muscovites to Mexican food.

There were a couple of feeble attempts to open up a Mexican food restaurant in Moscow. We were excited at the announcements, but soon discovered that opening Mexican restaurants in Moscow was like asking Northerners to cook fried okra, it just never tasted quite right. We decided we would stick with our own tried and true recipes. We decided that our first Russian guinea pig would be Andrei, our driver.

Robin used Russian flour and a sort of corn meal -- an ingredient which took several months to locate -- for creating the base for homemade soft tortillas for the enchiladas. She happened upon some avocados and lemons at the market and substituted leeks for onions to put together a mouth-watering dish of guacamole. The Spanish rice was easy, having brought a number of the traditional spices over from the States, since tomatoes and rice were plentiful.

I had heard that Mexican food can cause some people to perspire profusely. Since I had never observed the phenomenon personally, I was skeptical, but after seeing Andrei reach for napkin after napkin to wipe his forehead, I am now a believer. Once he tasted both the beef and cheese enchiladas, he couldn't get enough of them. We couldn't get him to stop. He would hold a soaked napkin to his forehead while continuing to shovel in the spicy food. In between bites, all he could utter was, "So good," in his dense Slavic accent.

We introduced Mexican food to other Russians as well. They seemed to enjoy the chicken fajitas, enchiladas, and the chips and salsa the best. They regularly told us it reminded them of Georgian food from the Southern regions, typically rich and spicy, which we took as a compliment.

Other rare treats we were able to purchase before they disappeared completely were canned pumpkin, soft bathroom tissue -- the Russian variety hurt too much -- a couple of six packs of an off-brand root beer, cranberry sauce, and a once in a lifetime seventy-five dollar turkey for Christmas dinner. Having invited over other friends stranded in Moscow for the holidays, we decided to go all out and create a memorable feast.

Humanity was well represented at our place on Christmas Day. We celebrated the holiday with a Russian, of course, an Egyptian, a Texas oil magnate, and a California businessman. As evening approached, we all sat down to a rousing game of Risk®. What a sight, six men and women from different parts of the world playing a game of world domination with pieces of plastic while eating pumpkin pie and listening to an old cassette of, "I'll Be Home for Christmas." I don't know if I'll experience another holiday like that one ever again.

11
SITTERS
SUPERSTITIONS
AND SANDWICHES

"Robin, come quickly. Lindsay is very ill. She must be taken to the *Poly Clinic.*" Olga, our regular sitter's mother filling in for her daughter, was frantic. She continued, "She has not moved. I cannot get her to wake up. She is so sick. We must take her now!"

Robin had just walked in the door from a day of shopping and was met face to face with an emergency. Olga was horrified, afraid that Lindsay, under her temporary supervision, was at the brink of death.

"Lindsay," Robin rushed into the living room calling out her name with fear and urgency. There she was, lying on the floor in front of the sofa, motionless, even lifeless. Robin scooped her up, her limp body draped over Robin's arms. "Lindsay," Robin shouted into her face.

"Seth, what happened?" Robin turned to him searching his expression for an answer.

We had been forewarned to exercise extreme caution when taking our family to a *Poly Clinic*. If we were ill, our best bet was to call an ambulance. Most ambulances possessed sterile syringes, a crucial item often found wanting in the Russian medical community. The hospitals and *Poly Clinics* could not be trusted as most of the medical practices were not only archaic, but often unnecessary.

I recall meeting a young man from Somalia who had just moved to Moscow to attend the University. Not feeling well for the first couple of weeks, thinking it might be the food, he finally decided to go to the local *Poly Clinic* for an examination. The physician discovered a large tapeworm and immediately scheduled the young student for exploratory surgery. The doctor wanted to extract the tapeworm by means of a scalpel. The day before the young student was to go under the knife, an American friend interceded, providing him with the proper oral medication killing the parasite, avoiding the unnecessary surgery. Instances such as this were not that uncommon.

Ambulances can also be hired as taxis, if they're not en route to an emergency. If you flag one down, you could find yourself taking a brief detour by way of the local *Poly Clinic* to drop a patient off for treatment before reaching your destination. We would see ambulances driving around the city on the lookout for healthy passengers in order to make a little extra money on the side. If they had the time, the drivers didn't take advantage of people in their time of need.

We first learned of the practice when two young Russian women offered to take Seth and Lindsay to the zoo. They promised to take good care of them and have them back by dark. Upon their return, Seth was ecstatic about his trip in the ambulance. The sitters calmed our fears, assuring us this was a common practice in Moscow. They would do just about anything for an extra *ruble.*

"Mommy, I think she's playing dead," Seth said with a five-year-old's degree of certainty.

"Oh no, she is not playing," Olga assured us. "She has not moved for a long time. I have tried to wake her. She will not respond. We must take her now."

"Lindsay, are you playing dead?" Robin demanded with a mother's authority.

Lindsay lifted up her head, opened her eyes for just a brief moment and said, "Uh huh," and then closed her eyes and dropped back into her limp and lifeless state.

Olga looked in disbelief. "How can this be?"

"Lindsay, stop playing dead this instant," Robin said.

"Okay." Lindsay leaped out of Robin's arms and headed off for her bedroom to play with her dolls.

"I'm sorry for this," Robin said.

"I, too, am so sorry," Olga said, embarrassed that she

was not able to discern play from real life in a two-year-
old.

The lack of success Russian sitters seemed to have
with American children stemmed from an even deeper
struggle.   I observed on numerous occasions that
Russian women refuse to say "no" to children. The five
Russian sitters we worked with did not have the word
"no" in their vocabulary. No matter how we tried to
elaborate on the rules for the day to the sitter, and then
instructed the kids not to take advantage of the sitter
while we were gone, all it took was one drawn out
"please" and a cute blink of the eyes, and the sitter
would cave in.

We got to know several sitters quite well over the
months. When we probed, trying to understand why
they would never correct or insist that the kids obey
them, they always came back with the same response,
"Your children are so beautiful. We could never say no
to their wishes."

Observing how Russians reacted to American children made us feel self-conscious. To me, Seth and
Lindsay are the most beautiful children ever, but they're
probably not in the running for the future Mr. and Miss
America. Seth has blond hair and deep blue eyes.
Lindsay has ash-brown hair with sparkling green eyes.
They are both pure extroverts. What was disheartening
about Russians, both strangers and friends, were their
comments about Seth and Lindsay's American looks,
with the added the phrase, "compared to Russian chil-

dren." It just wasn't the case, but there was no way to change their minds on the issue. We tried attacking the presupposition more than once, but they always countered with, "Yes, I believe Russian children are pretty, but they are not beautiful as your children are." Robin concluded that it must have been the confident and joyful demeanor of our children that brought on such comparisons.

Russians distinguished significantly between the treatment of boys and girls with boys receiving the best. Russian sitters had an especially soft spot for little American boys.

On Robin's shopping days, for example, when she was gone the better part of a day, she would make every effort to leave clear, precise instructions with the sitter as to what the children were to eat. In an effort to make things easier for everyone, she would prepare their lunches ahead of time. Every single time, upon our return, we discovered that Seth had gotten the pre-prepared lunch and anything else that was in the fridge or cupboard. They even encouraged him to take something a little extra. After this happened the fourth or fifth time, Robin started to become frustrated. The Russian sitter's response was always the same, "He is such a big strong boy. He needs to eat to be healthy. How could I say no? He was still hungry."

Of all the sitters we had throughout the year, only one caused any us serious difficulties. Her name was Irina. She had been with us for three months before we discovered her sticky fingers. Apparently she would routinely set the children up in the living room with a game to keep them preoccupied, and then pilfer our bedroom. We had brought over with us a year's supply of medical and cosmetic necessities. The only place we could store them were in the bookcases in our bedroom. She found our stockpile and began taking things from the very back of the shelf and then rearranging everything to look normal. After a while, Robin noticed that she seemed to be using up more of her makeup than anticipated and she was wondering if the year's supply was going to be enough.

We probably would have never discovered the missing items if it hadn't been for an eyebrow pencil inadvertently falling out of Irina's purse onto the floor. Upon further investigation we found aspirin, non-aspirin pain reliever, mascara, and base powder. When Irina discovered that we had found the cosmetics, she suddenly became too busy to watch the kids. We had planned to sit and talk with her about the incidents to see if we could better understand her reasoning, but she continued to cancel our appointments at the last minute. Her dismissal ended up being a mutual thing. Irina went to on to work at a new casino in Moscow. Knowing her family personally, we feared for her safety. If she thought she was taking a chance with the law by stealing cosmetics, she was in for an even bigger surprise. Her mother and father also were fearful that she may have gotten in over her head. We never saw Irina again.

We were thankful that all but one of our sitters were prone to spoiling and not stealing. If anything, they paid too much attention to the kids. I think they were fascinated by the interaction we had encouraged with Seth and Lindsay. Our sitters regularly commented on how we related with our children. "It is amazing to hear such good English come out of their mouths." "You treat them like adults." "You speak to them as if you expect them to understand you." These were some of the statements we heard over and over again from our sitters.

We noticed that Russian parents seemed to treat their children quite differently than American parents. Many Russian parents assumed we were doing a very poor job of taking care of our kids, until Seth and Lindsay would initiate a conversation and speak with respect to an adult. More than once Robin left Russian moms on the playground with mouths gaping, caught off guard that a child could interact intelligently with an adult.

In spite of this, Robin still found herself being scolded regularly on the playground, nearly to the point of being run off by a group of shouting, overly-protective mothers, about Lindsay's lack of warm clothes when outside. Russians believed that if a part of your skin was exposed to the cold air, you would become ill. If you put ice cubes in your drink, you would develop a sore throat. If you opened a window when there was a breeze, warm or cool, you would catch a cold. If you ate ice cream while it was cold outside you would come down with a chest infection. If a woman sat on cold ground, she would develop a female infection.

In a country with such a long history of dealing with inclement weather, it was amazing to find such phobias. Russians tended to ignore the danger of sharing germs, often drinking from the same glass without giving it a second thought. Surely the stifling heating systems and tropical conditions in the middle of winter contributed to illnesses as well.

I'm sure Russians viewed us as superstitious also. We could see the disapproval in their eyes when we refused to use a public restroom for sanitary reasons, preferring Seth and Lindsay relieve themselves behind a bush rather than risk exposure to a disease infested toilet that hadn't been flushed, much less cleaned, recently. We could see the disapproval in their eyes when Robin chose to carry bottled water everywhere, refusing to use public drinking fountains. Without pressure, the water would trickle down the side of the peeling chrome faucet, forcing you to place your lips on the exposed steel and suck with all your might. We refused to taste a special drink from a common cup shared with strangers at the local market. We refused to take a bite of a deformed apple plucked from a tree that had been planted decades earlier at a busy intersection.

We each had our own share of phobias and superstitions. Both sides were more than willing to enlighten the other, although neither was able to convince the other to change their thinking.

Most Russian mothers dote on their kids oppressive-ly, suffocating them into their teenage years, allowing little or no room for relational development in early life. I heard very few children actually interact with their parents. I rarely saw a father involved in the parent-child relationship until the child was much older. It seemed the children were to be seen, not heard.

Moscow has some of the brightest children in the world educationally, yet many appear underdeveloped in their relationships. I believe that was one reason the sitters loved our kids so much. They continually looked forward to the children's interaction with them. And of course, the kids always looked forward to the undivided attention they received.

Although we were never able to get through to a sit-ter the importance of being stern when necessary, we could rest assured that Seth and Lindsay would be well cared for. With a little creativity on our part, like hiding all the snacks in the compartment under the bathtub and boxing up things that Seth might want to eat beyond his lunch and placing them in our bedroom behind our new lock and key, we had a wonderful relationship with our sitters.

12
PETS
PUNCHES
AND PLAY BALL

"Um, ball *pazhalusta?* [please]" trickled a familiar young voice through the two heavy doors. I began the ritual of unbolting the fortress.

Twelve boys and two girls of all shapes and sizes, dressed in mismatched summer clothes, crowded around the door in the narrow hallway, all seeking to get a peek at how Americans lived. With smiles on their faces, they were ready to play.

"*Pyat minuta* [Five minutes]," I said. They nodded and hit the stairs at a sprint, no elevators for those athletes. America's favorite pastime was quickly becoming Russia's newfound obsession.

The children in our neighborhood had never seen a bat or a baseball until my five-year-old son, Seth, and I hit the playground in early June. At first, Seth and I took turns just hitting the ball to each another, chasing it on weird bounces and bad hops. The crumbling blacktop, the only smooth surface for blocks, made us wonder if it was worth packing the bat and ball.

Out for their daily dose of badminton, at the first crack of the bat the Russian children swarmed us. We asked them as best we could if they would like to give it a try. A few were too embarrassed and were content to watch, but the majority couldn't wait to take a swing at the ball.

We proved that day that baseball can be a universal sport, if you are willing to invest the time and effort. It transcends the language barrier, all you need is sign language.

We spent the rest of the day just letting them get the feel of the bat and baseball mitt. Since we only had two mitts to go around, the mittless kids did the best they could to stop the ball with their hands, their feet and the front of their shirt. The kids loved chasing the ball and throwing it back and forth. A ball hit to second base might have seven or eight relay throws back to the pitcher, just to keep the game interesting.

Teaching Russian boys and girls to bat was fun. Some were naturals, some weren't, but each had their own particular interpretation of what they were to do with the bat. Some held it high, others held it low. Some twisted the bat around their little bodies, others held it up stiff and straight. Some looked like they could tear the hide off the ball, others looked like they might start crying at any moment. All looked the bat over, admiring its feel at every curve. I smiled a lot, seeking to affirm their interest in the game with nods of approval.

Seth became the self appointed batting coach while I pitched to them. My five-year-old boy looked comical giving a twelve-year-old batting lessons. Seth is quite the ball player. When he was two and a half, I bought him his first tee-ball set. We set it up in the back yard and on his second swing, he hit it over the house. This five-year-old giving batting lessons was a natural at the game.

The older kids didn't quite know how to respond to instruction from a recent preschooler, so they politely ignored him and attempted to hit the ball on their own, trying to prove that they didn't need any help. But when their luck ran dry and they still hadn't connected, they always turned to Seth. He would smile and cheerfully say, "*Kharasho* [That's all right]." He would help them slide their hands up the bat, raise their back elbow up a little, and nod in approval. If they couldn't get it right, he would take the bat into his own small hands and show them how to perform a smooth swing with a good followthrough and then hand the bat back to them. They always responded shyly with a "*Spasiba* [Thank you]."

I recall a couple of young boys could really swing the bat and connect consistently, a little league coach's dream. But most would get so excited when they finally made contact that they would drop the bat and join in the race after the ball. Several of the girls decided to join in the exercise as well.

I recall one young girl in particular who shed her black leather jacket and cowboy boots -- one of two pairs I saw the entire year -- to take her turn. When she swung and missed, the boys waiting their turn behind her snickered and chuckled. She turned to them and said something in Russian that sent the look of death over their faces. Grins turned to fear.

After our day in the sun, a rare moment in Moscow, the kids begged us to come out again the next day. We nodded in consent and said over and over again, *"Da zaftra* [Until tomorrow]." The kids loved our feeble attempts to express ourselves. Several had taken some English in school and tried to speak with us in return. "Hi." "How are you?" and "My name is . . . " was about as far as they got. I realized that if we were going to teach those Russian youths the game of baseball, we were going to have to find some way to hurdle the communication gap.

The next day, our venture out to the playground was an anticipated event for all. Not only were the kids from the day before anxiously awaiting us, but many of their friends were there also. I remember speculating to Seth that we might be able to field two complete teams and have a real game of baseball.

We warmed up, tossing the ball around and taking a little batting practice. Seth, now in his familiar spot, was barking helpful hints for new pupils. He was prepared for the visual lessons as well. At one point, he gathered the children around himself and showed them in slow motion how to swing the bat. He then quickly jumped back into his coaching position, bent over slightly with hands on both knees with my oversized Mickey Mouse baseball cap pulled down over his ears.

It became obvious that everyone wanted to do more than just bat and chase the ball, but no one knew what to say or how to say it. Then I glanced over at Lindsay playing with a little Russian girl. They were drawing little faces, or so we were told that's what they were, on the blacktop with some form of sidewalk chalk. I asked the girls if I could borrow some. When the boys saw what it was I wanted, they started pulling huge chunks of the crumbling substance out of their pockets. It was going take all they possessed in order to map out a baseball diamond.

"*Adin, dva, tri, dom* [One, two, three, home]." I took the players on an excursion around the newly drawn baseball diamond. We walked around the outlined bases the first time. We ran the second time. Then I had Seth pitch to me. I hit the ball and ran to first. From that point on, we were forced to rely upon body language. With tremendous patience on both sides, we were able to explain that you stop at first if the ball is in the infield, that you didn't throw the ball at the runner, instead, you throw it to the person standing on the base, and that you had to run to the next base once the batter hit the ball. With my trusty chalk, I marked on the blacktop where each player was supposed to stand. Once they caught on, there was always someone standing in a particular spot, he wouldn't leave it, even for a ball hit just to the left or right of him within easy reach. He would just stare at the ball passing him by, wishing he could join in the fun chasing after it. The American coach had given him a responsibility; man the spot now marked and don't vacate it for any reason, was their interpretation. I also marked left, right and center fields and placed a player in each spot, hoping they would not take the marked spot as literally as our infielders did.

Perhaps the biggest hurdle was teaching the concept of three strikes, three outs, and three bases, all called the same thing, *adin, dva, tri* [one, two, three]. When I would say, "*Adin*," for strike one, the batter might run to first, assuming that I was telling him to head for first base. When I would say, "*Dva*," for out number two, the batter might run to second base, assuming that I was telling him to head for second. It took three or four mock games to teach them the difference between strikes, outs and bases. Over the next few weeks, before the rainy season hit, we were able to get in a couple of real games. Seth's team was the Chicago Cubs. He was always Mark Grace, his favorite player, although he didn't play first, nor was he left-handed.

I will probably never fully know the impact Seth and I had on those boys and girls, but someday one of them might become a professional baseball player and attribute some of his inspiration to an American father and son who took a few weekends out of their schedule to show him the game of baseball. Even if that were to never happen, Seth and I will always cherish the memories of Saturday afternoons in Moscow on a dilapidated playground temporarily turned makeshift baseball park, sharing the game we love with complete strangers. For a while we had the ability to erase things that divided, and instead, united two distinct cultures.

Seth and I weren't the only popular ones in our neighborhood. Robin had her own crowd of admirers. They ranged from two to twelve years of age, young Russian girls starved for attention and affection. Robin made her first appearance on the preschool playground right outside our flat. As she began to play games with Lindsay, the other girls noticed and began to flock around her, seeking the same interaction. The rest of the mothers just sat on their park benches and stared in disbelief, that a grown woman would consent to play children's games. Robin didn't care, and the kids loved her for it. They even taught her a few games of their own. Lindsay made some new friends, and initially, I'm sure, some of the attraction was due to the relatively new American toys she played with and was so willing to share.

Playing games with the young girls became a regular occurrence. Just as the new team of rookies would knock on our door asking to play ball, the girls would ask if Robin could come out and play. I'm sure her willingness to get involved in the lives of the Russian children was the subject of many a dinner table's conversation. Moms and dads looking on seemed intrigued by the fact that we weren't just supervising, as was the custom, but we were playing with them, and enjoying it too.

The only real threat on the playground were the dogs who loved to chase the balls and play with the toys, but were unwilling to share. We saw some of the most beautiful pure bred dogs in the world. There seemed to be very few mixed breeds. Russians have managed to create a network of pets that would rival our best show kennels. It was obvious how much they cared for their animals as they often treated them as well as their own children.

Every day, Andrei, our driver, was forced to scurry home in the early evening before picking me up from work, in order to prepare dinner for his dog, a pure bred German Shepherd. Each night he would cook his dog a two-course meal, usually rice and meat. We asked him why he didn't just feed it regular dog food, saving the lengthy preparation. He told us the Russian dog food was no good and the American dog food was too expensive. The rice and meat were cheap enough and could serve two purposes. Andrei could prepare extra so that he could feed his whole family and his wife wouldn't have to cook another dinner, and it would keep his dog healthy.

Russians were very protective of their dogs. As beautiful as the animals were, they provoked some of the most violent reactions I have ever observed between human beings. People would erupt into shouting matches with each other over their pets. More than once, I saw men get into fist fights over their four legged idols.

I remember sitting by our window on a Sunday evening, watching the CD player and hearing two men arguing below on the children's playground. They seemed to be taking turns casting aspersions at each other, hurling Russian slurs about the other's lack of culture, the ultimate Russian insult. Sensing the tension four floors above the argument, I expected it to escalate into a knife or gun fight. Watching from above, I noticed that they each had a dog on a leash. During their shouting match, they would point to the other's pet as if they were judging each other's social status according to the breed of their dog. At one point, the dogs got close enough to check each other out, sniffing their underside. In a rage, one of the owners reared back and punched the other man as hard as he could right in the mouth, knocking him to the ground, then reached down as if to console his violated animal, sneering at the fallen man, daring him to retaliate.

Not only did Russians idolize their pets, and relish their free time, but they also loved celebrations of any kind, and if they could find a way to make it a holiday from work, they would. Numerous times during each year, the city of Moscow put on wonderful fireworks displays. They occurred regularly throughout the summer and could be quite beautiful, once we got used to them. Rarely did we hear about an event before we "heard" the event. Sitting in a Russian flat, in a city of unrest, where might seems right, hearing nearby explosions could be disconcerting.

I recall our first experience as it lit up the northern sky. At the sound of the first explosion, we ran to the window. All we could see from our flat was the periodic flash of white light off the building that faced our kitchen window, then came the loud boom a few seconds later. My first thoughts were of the possible radiation from the attack and what would happen to Robin and the kids?

Several times we went to bed with the sky exploding and the ever present threat of civil war on our minds, not knowing whether it was for show or for real. Everyone we called failed to answer their phone, they were probably at the fireworks display. Turning our eyes away from the bedroom window, we always managed to fall asleep, praying everything would be okay.

Our leisure time took us on a number of outings in surrounding neighborhoods in search of something unusual or interesting to do or see. Although not as bold as my co-worker, who, for ten dollars, parachuted every Saturday during the summer at a local airport, we did have one brush with danger.

I had promised Seth and Lindsay that we would walk down *Vernadskova* to a small lake located next to a high-rise building. From the road, the walk around the lake looked harmless, but up close we discovered burned out cars, which Seth found fascinating, and numerous gangs of Middle-Easterners scrutinizing everyone as they passed by, as if they were looking for someone to pester.

Keeping a watchful eye on them, we hastily turned the corner of a small storage building, heading down to the water's edge. As we passed the building, a door was flung open and out walked seven teenagers in fatigues with automatic weapons. Leading them was an older man, shaven from head to toe. We quickly stepped out of their path, for fear that they would walk right over us. Seth looked on with eyes bulging, having never seen such young boys with such big guns before. Keeping their eyes focused straight ahead, they didn't even acknowledge us. They passed right by, disappearing into some tall grass and then up over a little knoll. I had no idea what they were doing or where they were going, but if they were going to step out on to *Vernadskova* and hop on a trolley, I'm glad we missed that one. Needless to say, our walk around the lake was a brisk one.

After that outing, I never complained about that crumbling blacktop Russians called a playground again. In fact, it didn't look half bad, as long as we could keep the dogs at bay.

13
EDUCATION
ENDANGERMENT
AND AN EARFUL

"If you desire the safety of your children, it will take more money," threatened the school bus driver. "If you do not pay me more, I cannot guarantee their return. The streets of Moscow are very dangerous these days."

This all too familiar conversation got old quickly. Everywhere we turned we heard, "It will cost you more money." Now our children's safety depended upon our being able to cough up enough to satisfy the driver's greedy appetite.

In early summer, we began to seriously consider placing Seth in a Russian grade school for the approaching fall semester. If we had come across a Russian teacher who spoke English and offered to take him on as a special project, we might have been persuaded. But that didn't happen. We made a difficult decision, after our experience with the local *Dietski Sod* [Russian kindergarten], to send Seth to a small, private, English-speaking school for children of missionaries. At least it was affordable. We couldn't justify sending him to the larger, more expensive American Embassy School. Ten-thousand dollars seemed steep for a kindergartner, even for our child.

We had heard from a friend that the *Dietski Sod* near our flat had several openings for four and five-year-olds for the summer. Their son had attended the school and seemed to enjoy it. We were told the teacher spoke English and welcomed the opportunity for English speaking children to attend her classes. Although we were told that the school was very popular and usually had a waiting list, the recent price increase for enrollment sent many families packing, searching elsewhere for a cheaper education. The ten dollars a month tuition was more than most average Russians could afford. After meeting with the Russian teacher and discussing the program, we consented to let Seth attend. He had been bouncing off the walls for months and was ready for kids his own age.

Seth's first day of *Dietski Sod* was a memorable one. They had asked, actually insisted, that he arrive twenty minutes early every day. That wasn't a problem since the school was on the way to work, so I could drop him off and observe his interaction with the Russian children.

His teacher was waiting for him with open arms. Although her English was very poor, her smothering affection and attention would easily win Seth over. The teacher explained to me that the children would have certain rules and rituals to perform every day. It was expected that Seth would be no different. She assigned him his own little locker where he would put his jacket and shoes. The kids were not allowed to wear shoes while inside. Each child had a mat assigned to them for their daily nap, in their underclothes. All the children, boys and girls, stripped down to their skivvies during nap time. At first, it sounded kind of risqué, but soon we discovered that it was a part of their daily routine and they didn't think twice about it. We decided we shouldn't either.

Seth's teacher asked him if he was hungry. Seth responded with a resounding, "Yes!" and then added, "What do you eat here?"

"Come, let me show you," the teacher said, taking his hand and leading him into the large, white room.

In the center of the room were three small wooden tables. Each table had eight tiny chairs around it. At each chair, there was a placemat with a spoon and a napkin. Several children were already seated, staring quietly at their new classmate. Several more kids entered the room and found their assigned seat.

"We serve you breakfast every morning," said the teacher. "You will come early so you may eat with us. You must have energy for the day."

Seth was willing to give it a shot, at least once, and found a place next to a cute little Russian girl with an oversized bow in her hair. He introduced himself with a congenial, "Hi, I'm Seth," but got no response. She just stared at him, dumfounded, unable to speak.

"Where's the other English speaking children?" I asked the teacher.

"Oh, they are away for the summer. Seth will be our only English speaking child. I am sure he will do fine."

I pulled Seth aside and quickly explained the situation to him. I asked him if he was comfortable with the arrangement. He wasn't interested in going back to his two-year-old sister and our tiny flat. It was a new adventure and there were lots of kids. Seth wouldn't have it any other way and returned to his seat, trying once again to befriend his classmates.

Just as I was getting ready to leave, two large Russian women walked through the door wearing faded white gowns and what appeared to be sterilized caps. "Oh no, not nurses," I uttered to myself, having already decided that Seth would pass on the Russian physical exam. They were actually the cooks, at least in a loose sense of the word. In the Pacific Northwest they have mush, in the Midwest they have Cream 'O Wheat, in the South they have grits. Kids in Moscow receive a daily dose of porridge with lukewarm goat's or cow's milk, whichever is available at the time.

Seth, our eating machine, only dabbled in the stuff. He couldn't get used to it, and I didn't blame him. Some days the porridge was hot, some days it was ice cold, some days it was overcooked, some days it was raw. He never knew what to expect. Nevertheless, he had to be there early, seated in his assigned chair. He had to pretend that he had taken a bite or two, then convince them he was full.

Things seemed to move right along. Seth was learning a lot of Russian and making new friends. Before we left the States, we purchased a couple of dozen Matchbox cars to give away as gifts. *His Dietski Sod* was the perfect opportunity to expose the other children to an American toy. Seth carefully picked out each car for each child and surprised them with his little gift. It was obvious some of the children had never received such a gift, and the Russian parents insisted that their children thank Seth every morning.

A couple of months into the summer session, Robin received a phone call one afternoon. The teacher seemed very upset and demanded to speak with me personally. Robin asked if something was wrong and if she could be of assistance. No, the teacher insisted on speaking with Seth's father. She confirmed that Seth was okay, but she needed to discuss something of importance with me immediately.

"Seth has done a terrible thing," the teacher began.

"What did he do?" I asked.

"As you know, Mr. Furmanek, we have an aquarium in our school. It has many beautiful fish in it. This afternoon, after the children's daily walk, Seth came back into the classroom, put his hand in the aquarium, grabbed a fish, pulled it out and tore it in half."

"What?" I said. "I don't believe it, not Seth. He loves

creatures of all kinds."

"It is true, Mr. Furmanek, but this is not all. I apologize for the actions of my assistant," she continued. "She has been dismissed for her part in this."

"Could you elaborate?"

"Today my assistant was with the class while I was at the University. She had taken them out on their daily walk around the neighborhood. While on the walk, Seth and another boy began to fuss about a stick lying on the street they both wanted. The older boy pushed your son, and in return, your son pushed him back. My assistant grabbed both of them by their arms in an attempt to break up the argument. Mr. Furmanek, she does not speak English. She could not understand your son, nor could your son understand her. When she would not let him go, your son told her to *pashol von* [a very rude way of saying 'get lost']. In reaction to this, my assistant slapped your son across the face. He cried for a short time and when they returned to class, he killed the fish."

The teacher was obviously distraught. She continued, "I am very sorry for all this and I have taken action to immediately correct the situation."

After a brief conversation, we both agreed that I would talk with Seth and see if there was any more to the story. I assured the teacher that Seth would be buying the school a new fish out of his allowance. We consented to discuss the matter further the following day.

The drive home gave me time to cool down. More embarrassed than angry, I was determined to get to the bottom of the matter. *Tearing a fish in half,* I thought, *what was going on in his little mind?*

I briefly explained the incident to Robin and went into Seth's bedroom where he was playing.

"Can you tell me what happened today?" I said.

"I'm sorry, Daddy." He jumped up and ran over to me and began to sob uncontrollably.

"Why don't we start at the beginning?" I suggested as I scooped him up into my lap.

"This boy pushed me," sniff, sniff, "because he wanted the stick I had and I wouldn't give it to him."

"Was it your stick?"

"No, it was lying on the street."

"Then what happened?"

"The other teacher grabbed me," Seth said excitedly. "And she wouldn't let me go."

"What did you do then?"

"I tried to get away. She was hurting me. Every time I moved she yelled at me in Russian. She kept on yelling louder and louder, but I couldn't understand her."

"Then what?"

"I told her what you and mommy always tell the gypsies, *pashol von.*"

"Do you understand that was wrong?" I said, while grinning under my breath, amazed at what he had picked up from us.

"Yes, and I won't ever do it again," Seth assured me, breaking down once again.

"Is that why she slapped you?" I said.

"Yes. She was mad at me."

"Is that why you killed the fish?"

"Yes, sir."

"Do you realize that you will have to buy them another fish out of your allowance?"

Seth wiggled off my lap, walked over to his piggy bank, picked it up and handed it to me. It broke my heart, and it was obvious there was something more there, so I continued. "Can you tell me about your day at school? How do you like the teacher?"

"Daddy, I don't think I want to go back to that school. The teacher who used to talk to me in English is never there anymore."

"What?" I said. "She's supposed to be there every day."

"Daddy, she hasn't been there in a long time."

"Why do you think you killed the fish?"

"I couldn't talk to anyone. No one speaks my language and I don't speak theirs. I can't understand the things we're supposed to do and they get mad at me for that."

I gave Seth a big hug and told him that I forgave him, but that he was still going to have to replace the fish.

"Could you please explain why you haven't been teaching the classes?" I asked, settling deep into a chair, preparing for long conversation. I had brought Andrei, my driver/interpreter, along with me for understanding and clarification.

"Mr. Furmanek, as you know, things are difficult in Moscow," she began deliberately. "I cannot make enough money to live just working at the school. I must do other things. My tutoring has taken me to the University. I can make much money there."

During our conversation I discovered that she had been showing up at the school only once or twice every two weeks. As a result, Seth hadn't been able to talk with anyone during the majority of his schooling, yet he didn't complain. When asked how school was, he always replied, "Oh, Great." I'm sure the unemployed assistant became just as frustrated as he had.

She was very apologetic for the assistant's actions. She acted nervous, perhaps fearful we would call the *Militsiya* for misconduct. I assured her that we wouldn't take any action and that Seth would apologize for being rude. We agreed that it would be best for Seth to attend only on the days that she would be there. Expecting a five-year-old to attend a school where he couldn't talk to anyone was too much to ask.

He finished out the summer with no further problems. In fact, he became so popular that they wanted him to return for the fall semester. After discussing it with Robin, and discovering that the teacher would no longer be with the school, we decided it would be best to do something else.

Luckily we were able to find a small, relatively inexpensive elementary school for Seth to attend. Coming from a Christian background ourselves, the Christian school for the children of missionaries was going to be a welcome change. We would be the first family with a business background whose children would be allowed to attend.

Seth enjoyed his class of twelve. There were children from all parts of the world with their own stories to tell, but they all spoke English. The elementary school was located in a Russian high school. Both schools coexisted throughout the school year, sharing common areas as needed. The elementary school's administrative offices were housed in a couple of converted, yet still rundown, flats near the school. With the overpopulation of the school, there were no offices available.

Though the school was just what we needed, the stresses brought on by Seth's lack of transportation were a weekly issue. Getting him to school and back safely became a monumental problem.

The school was located on the Outer Ring Road, sixteen bus stops beyond the end of the Metro line. The drive took forty-five minutes to one hour each way. The parents in our district had decided to pitch in and hire a bus driver, then another, then another, and then another. The drivers usually lasted only a week or two. No matter who they were or where they came from, they always arrived at the same conclusion, more money would make everything safe for the children. Robin began to receive phone calls every Friday, like clockwork, from the mother coordinating the transportation, informing us that we had lost another driver, but that they had found another company who would begin on Monday.

After depleting the list of bus drivers in Moscow, we were told everyone was to resort to car pooling. Being the only family in our district with only one school aged child, we thought it would be easy for Seth to hitch a ride with someone else. No such luck, the network of missionary families had already made their arrangements. We would have to fend for ourselves.

After three months of struggling, fretting, and praying daily about how to get Seth to and from school in some regular fashion, our driver broke down and consented to begin to take Seth to school. The money wasn't the issue, for we offered that early on. I think he truly felt sorry for us. Perhaps he had seen Robin break down weeping one too many times when Seth's bus or taxi failed to show up, or drove right past while they waved frantically attempting to catch the driver's attention. Whatever the cause, we were thankful for his help. All we had to worry about was Seth arriving to school on time and that seemed minor in light of our recent escapades.

Through all the bumps and bruises, all the chaos and catastrophes, I think the educational experience was worth it. There are not too many American children who can say that they have attended school in Russia, much less a Russian school where they were the only English speaking student. We were blessed, though at times we felt as if we had been cursed.

14
NEW YEAR'S NEIGHBORS AND NEANDERTHALS

In Moscow, holidays were what we made of them. There were no television specials or commercials to foster the mood. There were no neighborhoods decked out in Christmas lights to drive through. Santa Claus does not temporarily set up shop in the local mall. There are no department stores dedicated to the holiday shopper, no restaurants filled with families sitting down for a meal after Church, dressed in their Sunday best. Russia could be a winter wonderland and an emotional wasteland, simultaneously. Since being far from our extended family and holiday traditions was now second nature, we were forced to develop a number of our own family traditions.

Christmas in Russia is celebrated on January 7 according to the Orthodox Church Calendar. In 1993, Easter was celebrated a week later than it was by the Protestant Church in America. Russians don't celebrate

Memorial Day, Independence Day, Labor Day, or Thanksgiving Day.

When the first holiday rolled around, things seemed to be just a little off kilter, but rather than drown in self-pity, Robin suggested that we take advantage of the opportunity and enjoy each holiday in our own way, celebrating Easter and Christmas twice. The kids loved the idea, having Christmas twice in one year. Robin's spirit and creativity made all of our holidays a celebration.

"Rick, when someone gives you an egg at Easter, it is a very special gift," Andrei explained, handing me the dark brown, yet finely decorated, hard-boiled egg. "You must put it in a special place for the Easter season," he continued. "It will bring you good luck. Then you must eat it."

I carefully placed the egg in a small bowl on the table in the hallway, near the door for all to see. I thanked Andrei for the gift and gave him the traditional Russian sign of affection, a kiss on the left cheek, a kiss on the right cheek, and another kiss on the left cheek. When a Russian gives you a gift, you shouldn't take it lightly, no matter how small. We made every attempt to show deep appreciation to anyone who offered us something, whether it be food, hazardous to our health or not, or a book, a favorite gift Russians love to give.

There was one gift we received on the Russian Easter that truly humbled us. We didn't realize the significance of the Easter gift Valentina, our elderly next door neighbor, gave us until the holiday was long passed.

We were finishing our second Easter dinner when the doorbell buzzed. Valentina identified herself in her familiar way, "Um, Valentina. Open the door,"

In her hands were two beautiful plates, each with what appeared to be a cake, or pastry placed neatly in the middle. She flashed her golden smile from ear to ear and immediately headed for our kitchen, all the while jabbering in Russian. We had learned to just nod and smile. She set each plate in the middle of the tiny kitchen table and stepped back, admiring her handi-work. The cakes or pastries looked beautiful. We were honored that she would go to such trouble to prepare something like this for us. We did our best to show our appreciation, but she seemed intent on expressing to us the importance of finishing all of the goodies she brought over. She did so with a more serious insistence, not her usual grandmotherly style. We offered her the traditional Russian kiss, which made her day, and the kids gave her their daily dose of hugs and pecks on the cheek. She left, still preoccupied with our understand-ing that we must eat all of the cake and not throw any of it away.

Andrei explained to us later that the two dishes Valentina gave us were two Russian traditions shared with family during the Easter celebration. The cake was called a *kulich*, a round risen loaf with raisins and icing, the mound of white on the other plate was called a *pash-ka*, a molded dish of eggs, sugar and curd cheese. Most

Russians now purchase these baked goods, readily available in Russian stores during the Easter season. Few Russians still prepare the *kulich* from scratch and even fewer Russians ever attempt to make the *pashka* since they can be expensive and time consuming. They also require knowledge and talent in the kitchen.

Valentina always made both baked goods from scratch, a long tradition in her family. It was no small expense for her family, though. Oleg, her husband, retired from the University, received a pension of twenty-five to thirty dollars a month. They didn't have a lot of extra *rubles* to spare, yet they insisted on sharing with us. This was not, however, her reason for insisting on our thoroughness to the task of eating the cake.

Once baked -- traditionally on a Saturday -- Valentina took the *kulich* to Church with her on Easter morning for consecration, another Russian tradition. Before you eat the *kulich,* it must be blessed, or set apart, by the Priest, thus her concern. The seventy-five year old woman gingerly carried two *kuliches* to the bus stop, got on the trolley, went to Church and made it back. She told Andrei to tell us she wanted to do this as a sign of true friendship and blessing for our family.

Memorial Day, Independence Day and Labor Day came and went in an atypical quiet fashion. We ended up spending each of the holidays at home. If we attempted to plan an outing, it seemed our driver always had something else to do and was unable to be with us that day. So Robin would concentrate on preparing a special holiday meal, inviting friends and acquaintances over to share in the celebration. We would make games or crafts to emphasize the special day for the family. Our creativity and personal understanding of each holiday seemed to expand and deepen when we were separated from the traditions with our extended family. We closed each holiday with a phone call back to the States, wishing everyone the best, missing them deeply, yet having grown from the experience.

On Independence Day we were invited to the ex-pat company picnic at the Moscow Golf and Country Club. Loving golf, I looked forward to attending, even if just to see something that resembled a green. The company had arranged a Fourth of July fireworks display and a western-style barbecue with all the fixin's. At the last minute we had to decline due to Robin's severe allergies. It turned out to be a blessing in disguise. The fireworks display was a dud, the barbecue was drenched by a downpour and the Metro Mosquitoes were out in full force. Everyone I spoke with who attended said it was a miserable night.

Halloween rolled around and a company party was announced. This time, the thousand-plus employees, both Russian and American, were invited to attend. Robin seized the opportunity to create homemade costumes for Seth and Lindsay, so that we might enjoy a more full festive experience than our usual family gathering in our tiny Moscow flat. The festivities were to start right after work so it was agreed that Robin and the kids would meet me in my office. Having a pierced ear from earlier days, I dressed as a pirate with a large gold earring. Robin was a *GAI* [pronounced Guy-ee], the Moscow traffic cop. Seth was dressed as the CEO of the company and Lindsay went as an Indian Princess.

I don't know what we expected, but what we found wasn't it. As we entered the ballroom at the hotel, we discovered nearly every Russian employee was already drunk and it was only 6:00 p.m. The doors had been open only thirty minutes. The co-workers I had planned on introducing to my family were too intoxicated to meet them.

Three burly Russian men I worked with terrified Seth. They began punching on him, trying to egg him on to wrestle with them on the floor while shouting as loudly as they could in his ear. They couldn't figure out why a five-year-old wasn't responding to their fun and games. Fearful it was getting out of hand, I pried Seth out of their clutches, so they wouldn't hurt him in their drunken stupor. Seth and Lindsay turned to us, ten minutes into the party and asked if we could go.

"I don't like seeing all the drunk people," Seth said, wiping his eyes, tearfully disappointed that the party had turned out like it had.

We were expecting something fun and festive. Instead, we saw a fight break out and a drunk pass out on the floor. We stuck around only long enough for the costume contest, but that was about all we could stomach.

Thanksgiving came upon us in wintry silence. Most of the ex-pats had left for the States for the holidays. Having a family of four, we didn't have the extra five-thousand dollars for plane tickets. We began to feel as if we were stranded in Moscow, unable to leave even if we had wanted to.

We were told that most joint-venture companies in Moscow insisted that their ex-pat employees leave Russia every three or four months for a week or two. With the constant pressure of mixing Russian and American business styles, the daily policy challenges, and the growing despair of the society, many were concluding it was not healthy to remain for any extended period of time.

We were into our ninth month without a break, not even a four-day vacation. Having the family there as a diversion was helpful, but we were definitely beginning to feel the full impact of being isolated.

We found some relief when Shelley, Robin's sister, sent us a care package loaded with holiday decorations and presents. We were thankful no one had pilfered through the goods, as everything was pretty much intact.

Included in the care package were paper displays of pumpkins, turkeys, and a cornucopia. She even included a placemat from a Pizza Hut® and Taco Bell®, welcome touches of the familiar. She sent some holiday

M&M's® and goodies for the kids. There were some Christmas decorations too, but of course no tree. We were so thankful that we opened the box several times just to have the experience of receiving something from America again and again.

While we were there, the government began finding large numbers of oversized duffel bags full of letters and packages that had been dumped in a lake near the airport. It seemed a disgruntled postal worker, or hardline Communist, didn't want foreigners receiving anything. In the bags were checks, documents, transactions, and just about anything else people sent through the mail. After reading about that, we discouraged anyone from sending anything of importance through the Russian mail system.

As a gesture of goodwill, the company provided a Thanksgiving meal for those ex-pats left behind in Moscow. With no turkeys available for under fifty-dollars, we decided to take another chance and attend a company party. This affair was promised to be benign compared to the Halloween fiasco.

The room was filled with beautifully decorated tables. We mingled and made small-talk until it was time to take a seat. Everyone seemed preoccupied, even distant. The dinner quickly took on an air of sadness. Everyone conversed, appreciating a warm body to share the holiday with, but it was apparent all longed to be elsewhere with family and friends.

The turkey was wonderful, but the trimmings, cooked by a French chef, didn't even resemble a traditional Thanksgiving meal. The sweet potatoes didn't taste like sweet potatoes, the dressing didn't taste like dressing, the pumpkin pie didn't taste like pumpkin pie. It felt as if we were seated in a French restaurant, rather than grandma's dining room table.

After a dinner served with hushed small-talk, we quietly exited the room, unable to cope with the silence of the normally cheerful holiday. We thanked the coordinator of the dinner for his efforts and made our way home. March 15, the end of my contract, became our light at the end of the tunnel, yet it still seemed so far away. At that point we found ourselves struggling to be thankful on that special day of blessing. We simply felt empty and alone.

The Christmas season was upon us before we knew it. We had heard a rumor from overseas that we might receive a surprise present and be shipped home to the States for the holiday, but it was only a rumor. When the reality of spending Christmas in Moscow hit us, we decided that we needed to be proactive on the holiday front.

Unable to find a Christmas tree in Moscow for the December 25 celebration, Robin decided to build her own. Seth volunteered his tee-ball stand and Robin found some green construction paper. After three hours of carefully cutting, coloring, and taping, we had our first homemade Christmas tree. Primitive though it may have been, it served our purpose, a gathering place for worship, for presents and homemade decorations. We appreciated it that much more from the effort and challenges. Both Seth and Lindsay each made their own special decoration. Robin had collected a number of Russian Santas from the local souvenir shops, some carved out of wood, some porcelain and others made with clay. She transformed a small corner of our flat into a wonderful Christmas corner.

On Christmas Eve we read the traditional Christmas story and drank hot chocolate with lots of marshmallows. After dinner, we went down to the playground, fell back into the newly fallen snow and made snow angels.

Since that particular Christmas wasn't going to be characterized by lots of presents and overstuffed stockings, we seized the opportunity to teach the kids the importance and privilege of giving to others. We baked homemade breads, cookies, and pies together and delivered them to our neighbors, wishing them a *S razhdistvom Khristovym* [Merry Christmas with the birth of Christ.]. They appreciated the early gifts, their Christmas still being some two weeks away, and it gave them a chance to sample traditional American recipes such as brownies, chocolate chip cookies and banana nut bread. Valentina went wild over the brownies with walnuts. As far as Valentina was concerned, Robin was a miracle worker. Robin worked two miracles that I know of.

The first miracle was teaching Valentina, a seventy-five year old Russian *babushka*, how to make her own batch of brownies using only sign language. Robin visually showed her what to use and how much was needed while Valentina wrote down the recipe in Russian. It was also difficult for Robin, for she rarely bakes with a recipe. She is a gifted cook who throws things together empirically, if it looks right and feels right, she adds it.

Valentina actually got the brownie recipe down pretty good. She was so appreciative of the help that she returned the favor by preparing us several dozen brownies. Actually I think she was looking for approval from her teacher.

The second miracle was even more amazing. Valentina was mesmerized by our Russian microwave oven. She often described its capabilities to her daughter, longing to have one of her own, but knowing she and Oleg couldn't afford it.

For their fiftieth wedding anniversary, their entire family pitched in and surprised them with a microwave just like ours. Valentina was so moved and excited, she asked Robin to come over immediately and begin giving her cooking classes. Through a week of constantly, yet patiently, going back and forth from flat to flat, Robin was able to teach Valentina how to successfully use a microwave oven for everyday meal preparation, once again without any helpful verbal interaction.

With two children in the flat, Christmas came early, five a.m., and didn't end until well into the night. Robin fixed her famous blueberry muffins for breakfast and a pot of cinnamon coffee. We dressed for the day and began preparing the Christmas meal. We stuck the oversized, *ochin daragoy* [very expensive] turkey in the tiny oven and began to prepare all the trimmings. Keeping a watchful eye for six months, Robin was able to slowly collect nearly everything she needed to pull off a glorious Christmas feast.

We invited an Egyptian general manager, a Texas oil magnate, a California businessman, and a twenty-year-old Russian model with aspirations of becoming an actress to share our dinner. The kids loved the full flat, the attention and the holiday noise. We were determined not to have another repeat of Thanksgiving. We laughed, we joked, we shot darts at the face of the clock on the wall, and played Risk all evening. No one wanted to leave. It was a holiday worth remembering, spent with new friends, people we truly enjoyed but would probably never see again. We helped each other find a real touch of home that day.

There is one event that both Russians and Americans celebrate on the same day, at exactly the same time, every single year: New Year's Eve. Seth's birthday falls on New Year's Eve as well. It was tough early on getting through to him that all parties held on New Year's Eve were not in his honor.

While in Moscow we tried to make both the kid's birthdays memorable. I started their special day with chocolate chip pancakes and juice. We let them choose what they wanted to do for the day and both wanted birthday parties.

For Seth's birthday, we held a combination birthday party/New Year's Eve celebration. As a special treat, we told the kids that they could stay up until midnight to usher in the new year, if they could keep their eyes open.

The birthday party was a smashing success, ending about nine. After everyone left, we put on our night clothes and settled down for a movie, Seth's choice, which ended around eleven-thirty. After the movie was over, we encouraged the children to hang on just a few more minutes. Barely able to keep their eyes open, they had lost all excitement and asked to be put to bed. Giving in to their wishes, we put them down for the night. At eleven forty-five the doorbell buzzed. Robin and I looked at each other in amazement.

Had someone left something behind, I thought, scanning the room for anything unusual.

I walked over to the door and asked, "Who is it?"

"Um, Valentina. Open the door."

I glanced at Robin, and she was as surprised as I.

Shrugging my shoulders, I unbolted the door.

Valentina looked strikingly beautiful. Her snow white hair showed off a new hairdo. She wore a lovely dress with pearls. But the thing I noticed most of all was she was wearing makeup. She looked as if she were ready for a gala.

She was obviously excited about something.

"Um, *polnach* [midnight]," she said over and over, pointing at the clock.

Robin and I looked at her and smiled, but that wasn't what she was wanting to tell us. Hearing all the commotion, the kids jumped out of bed and latched onto Robin.

"Um, come," she said, grabbing my arm and pulling me out into the hallway. I began to think something might be wrong.

"Just a minute," I said, but that wasn't good enough.

"Um, *pashli!* [let's go!]" she insisted.

Looking around the room, frantically trying to find a way to express herself, all the while keeping a watchful eye on the clock, she looked down at my gym shorts. She reached over, grabbed them and tried to pull them down around my knees. I immediately jumped back, startled by her lack of modesty, but that didn't stop her. She reached for me again. I took another step back since I had nothing on underneath.

"I think she wants us to change clothes," Robin said.

I moved toward the door and looked out into the hallway. She appeared to think I was getting the idea.

She stepped out into the hallway and opened her door.

"I get it," I said. "She wants us to come over to her party and help ring in the New Year."

I asked her to give us five minutes.

We threw on some clothes, left the kids in their pajamas, and headed for a traditional Russian New Year's Eve celebration. We arrived just a couple of minutes before midnight.

We were introduced to Oleg and Valentina's daughter and son-in-law, and Valentina's mother who seemed to be in very good health for being over ninety-years-old.

Everyone was watching the Russian television, looking for the signal that the New Year was to begin. Oleg quickly poured everyone a small glass of Russian vodka for a toast. Once the announcement of the New Year's arrival was made over the television, everyone shouted *S novym Godam!* [Happy New Year!] and began walking around the room hugging and kissing each other. Then Oleg held up his glass for a toast. He wished everyone a long and happy life and drank. He poured everyone another small glass and proposed that I make the toast. I toasted to friendship. He tried to pour us another glass, but we had to decline. The vodka burned like nothing I had ever drunk before.

Once everyone was toasted out, the son-in-law lit a fountain, one of those fireworks that spews sparks three or four feet into the air, right in the middle of the table. I thought the place would go up in flames, but it looked like they had done it many times before. The kids loved seeing fireworks being set off inside a flat.

The table was set with beautiful china, and on the china rested a complete sit-down meal with exquisite foods from different regions of Russia. Having eaten our fill of homemade pizza and birthday cake earlier in the evening, sitting down to eat again, unique as it may have been, was going to be pure torture. There was no more room for food and drink.

Valentina seated everyone in their assigned place. Robin sat next to Valentina's daughter, decked out in a red satin dress, two or three sizes too small.

"Beautiful, no?" Valentina asked again and again.

"*Da, krasivy* [Yes, beautiful]," Robin responded again and again.

The food was interesting to say the least. There were rolled meats, fried meats, baked meats, raw meats, pickled meats and jelled meats. There was crab from the East Coast of Siberia, fish, pickled vegetables, and lots of caviar, both black and orange. A popular way of serving caviar in Eastern Europe was to place a spoonful of the fish eggs in a hard-boiled egg, sliced in half with the yoke removed. Instead of deviled eggs, you had deviled caviar.

Being as polite as possible, every time I tried to express I was full, Valentina would allow her fingers to trickle down her cheeks, suggesting that my refusal to eat more would make her cry. Then she would scoop up another spoonful of whatever was just eaten and place it on my already bulging plate.

Robin and I dabbled at the food, not wanting to discourage her gracious hospitality. It was a holiday, a time for celebration. After every bite, Valentina looked to us for approval.

"Mmmm," was our response at first, but that only encouraged her to add more to the plate. She refused to take no for an answer.

The bantering back and forth went on for over an hour. I was struggling to shovel down food, but out of courtesy, I was careful not to express it.

The kids flatly refused to taste anything but the desserts and there were all kinds to choose from. It was like sitting in a nice restaurant and having the server bring the dessert tray to you. Valentina wheeled a cart with three tiers housing luscious desserts into the dining room every fifteen minutes, insisting that everyone take another slice of cake or tort.

At one-forty a.m. we waddled back into our flat. We had gone into a food coma. Too bloated to lie down, Robin and I stayed up and watched another movie. Valentina had filled several large plates of food and sent them home with us for our hunger pangs the next day, but the hunger pangs never came.

15
GOD
GRACE
AND GRUDGES

Nothing I have ever experienced could prepare me for the pace of change we observed in Russia. Things, people, events, decisions, businesses, change on a dime. Rarely were people given adequate time to prepare or respond to the government's constant alteration of policy.

The Church in Russia was no different. The Russian Orthodox Church was also experiencing the growing pangs of change. I believe that if they don't begin to address the spiritual starvation of their society, a society also in transition, Russians will begin to look elsewhere for direction and meaning. In fact, many already had.

There was a curiosity about the spiritual world everywhere. Alongside the pornographic predator in the Metro, there might be someone peddling psychic or spiritualist writings just as fervently. The Metro was often inundated with flyers, each spiritual guru spread-

ing his or her own form of religion to anyone who
would give them a hearing. Thousands recently gathered in Kiev to follow a woman claiming to be a messi-
ah.

The new religious freedoms in Russia had provided
many new opportunities and many new temptations.
Religious groups with a bent for the sensational or the
lust for power found it easy to prey upon people who
were spiritually destitute and severely oppressed for
decades. Talking with Russians about their spiritual
experiences, I got the feeling many were disillusioned,
rarely receiving what was promised.

For the duration of our stay in Moscow, we attended
an English-speaking Church which primarily targeted
foreigners living in Russia. Through advertising in the
local English newspaper, the church also attracted a
number of metropolitan English-speaking Russians,
curious about American ways. Some attended only for
practicing their English skills, still others came interested
in the spiritual message.

We were fortunate to find the Church meeting where
it was supposed to be. Our experience taught us that
churches without a permanent building in Moscow did-
n't stay in one place for too long. I remember receiving
five or six leads from people in the States who knew, or
knew of, someone who attended a particular church in
Moscow. We were provided phone numbers and
addresses of contacts. When we called, attempting to
find out meeting times, it seemed all of them had van-

ished. We searched, networked, called back to the States for confirmation of numbers, and every time we struck out. We weren't able to find any of them.

The church seemed to attract people from all walks of life. When we left Russia, several hundred people from over twenty-two different nationalities were regularly worshiping together under one roof. It was a privilege to see and experience the different style of worship each person brought with them. On any given Sunday we would find professionals, diplomats, students and the homeless standing side by side. The contemporary approach to worship encouraged everyone to lay aside differences and experience God in their own way.

One family, in particular, remains in our thoughts, even to this day. A young Iraqi couple and their two small children showed up at a worship service one Sunday looking for assistance. Fearing their lives were in danger, the family had decided to flee Iraq and were now living underground in the Moscow Metro. The husband, trained as a biological chemist, was being coerced into assisting in Iraq's biological warfare program, but refused to participate. They were smuggled into Russia and were living there without passport or visa. If they approached the authorities for help, they were sure to be shipped back to Iraq.

The church became committed to providing a job for the husband and food and clothing for the family. The Iraqi family showed a genuine spirit of gratitude and appreciation. Because the church body had decided to invest in a long term relationship, the family was eternally touched and transformed. The last we heard, the family had made it out of Russia with new passports and visas and were starting a new life somewhere in Western Europe.

With so many different nationalities worshiping together in one place, we also were exposed to the sporadic, yet deep-seated, prejudice Russians have developed against Ukrainians. Even some of the Russian Christians on the worship team struggled with accepting the Ukrainian Christians.

The prejudice didn't end with the Church. The congregation was forced to move out of Lenin's Children's Library and into the Information Building located across the street from the *Park Kultury* Metro for a number of reasons, one being that we were allowing Ukrainians to worship with us. The Director of the Library and her staff detested our allowing Ukrainians into the building, even when the library was closed. We were forced to either move or ask the Ukrainians not to come back to church. We chose to move.

It was disconcerting to hear from foreign missionaries stationed in Moscow that it was a cinch to raise money in the States to start a church in Russia. The common thread running through each of the stories was this: Churches were more than ready to pay for people willing to go, just as long as they brought back stories of huge revivals throughout Eastern Europe. I recall a missionary I met whose financial support dried up because he refused to send back embellished reports of widespread conversion. His long term philosophy wasn't what his supporters wanted to hear. The money designated for his family's support went to someone else.

Some Americans who came over on short term missions took stories back to the States of great spiritual change sweeping Russia. What many didn't understand was that Russians could sit and politely listen to someone talk about their faith solely for the purpose of practicing their comprehension of conversational English, and they'll even nod and pray with you in agreement. Few Russians would seriously consider the ideas until they weighed all the ramifications.

The comments from young Russians who willingly shared their impressions with us after attending a large American-led crusade in Moscow seemed to reflect the general attitude toward religion.

"It was like the Communist Party meetings I used to attend when I was young. Everyone does the same thing, whether sitting or standing, at the same time."

"They make you sit while someone stands behind a podium and makes promises."

"It was just like the propaganda we received when we were Communists." "He told us to make a decision to give up everything and follow this Jesus. It reminded us of the coercion we received from our leaders to give up everything and follow their rules."

Russians required people to win the privilege of being heard and considered. Truth was a subjective concept to minds shaped by totalitarianism. The day to day fleshing out of truth was the penetrating difference to souls sealed by a lifetime of fear and false hope.

Russia took a tremendous risk allowing religious freedom in the face of the State Church's opposition. Intent on maintaining its firm grip on Russia's spiritual life, the Russian Orthodox Church did everything it could to curb the influx of new faiths. Once it became law, the Patriarchs made a number of unsuccessful overtures to the Government petitioning to be the only recognized Church allowed in the Country, and that all other Movements attempting to proselyte in Russia would first need to be approved by them. This has been denied thus far.

Is there value in true religious freedom? In a country unaccustomed to trusting its leaders, only time will tell.

16
CAGES
CALAMITIES
AND CLAUSTROPHOBIA

"Pamoch, pazhalusta [Help, please]," Robin shouted. "Can anyone let me out?"

Robin had stopped by our Pastor's flat to pick up some music for the following Sunday. She knew she was taking a chance using the elevator. In all our visits, it only seemed to work about ten percent of the time, but watching someone just climb out of it, she assumed it was a good day.

The metal cage had seen better days. It resembled a chicken coop rather than a transport for human beings. It smelled like a chicken coop too. The outer door was a mangled mass of twisted, deformed steel, and the gate handle was missing, leaving nothing to grasp. You could only put your finger in the jagged hole and pull it toward you, while trying to avoid being cut by pieces of protruding metal. Someone had torn off half of the inner door and carried it off. Luckily, the half that remained was the side that triggered the elevator.

Robin climbed in, managing to close the outer door without maiming herself, and swung the remaining half of the inner door shut while pushing the button for the fifth floor. The ancient pulleys and cables began to creak and groan, working against one another as the cage began inching upward, past the fifth floor, past the sixth, past the seventh, past the eighth. With a loud thud, the elevator slammed to a stop between the eighth and ninth floor. The light in the cab flickered once and went out, indicating the door wasn't shut all the way. Barren light sockets in the tiny hallways left everything pitch black. Opening and closing the inner door once again, Robin felt around for the button panel and pushed one. Nothing happened. She pushed another one. Still nothing. Quickly losing her composure, she began to frantically push all the buttons. She opened and closed the inner door again and again with no luck.

She began to cry out for help, mixing a little Russian with a lot of English. "Can anybody hear me? *Pamoch, pazhalusta* [Help, please]. Let me out. Help me someone! Can anyone let me out?"

Dogs in various flats began to bark behind their doors, some with deep woofs, others with high-pitched yips. Hearing the Russian owners quieting their pets, she yelled out again.

Then she heard the familiar sound of a fortress being unbolted. If she stood on her tip toes, she could see a faint sliver of light from one of the flats on the floor above. Someone was peeking out, trying to see what all the commotion was.

"*Pamoch, pazhalusta* [Help please]."

The door slammed shut. The dreadful sound of locks being latched once again began to torment Robin.

"Don't go, please, I need help," she cried out, becoming frightened, fearful that she might not get help. Two other doors were cracked open and slammed shut just as quickly.

The building became eerily still.

Out of desperation, she felt around for something to make some noise. In her belt pack she found her key ring with the many keys for each of the locks protecting our flat.

Feeling her way around the cage, she found the best spot to begin her noisy assault. In a single motion, she began to stomp her feet, sending a reverberating echo throughout the silent building, while raking her keys back and forth over the chain link cage. The dogs let loose again.

After several minutes of nonstop noise, a door flew open and a little *babushka* scampered out into the hallway. She approached the elevator, bent way over and peered between the two floors. Looking down into the cage, she could see only a portion of Robin's head.

The *babushka* barked a couple of instructions to Robin, which she couldn't make out. All she could do was stare up at the tiny woman, now squatting nearly on her hands and knees, in order to get a better look.

She spoke again. Robin just looked at her and said, "*Ya nye panimayu* [I don't understand]."

The little *babushka* was tenacious, refusing to give up. She began to describe with body language that Robin needed to pull on something. She began feeling around in the cage, her eyes now used to the dark. The faint light from the flat only revealed ghostly shadows. She looked up again. The woman kept pointing to something and pantomiming as if she was pulling on it.

Desperate, Robin began pulling on anything she could put her hands on, bolts, wires, buttons, and doors. Suddenly, the elevator rocketed downward. The little woman continued jabbering at Robin as the cage descended down, down. Robin sent a resounding echo through the building, "*Spasiba* [Thank you]," setting the dogs loose again. The elevator rocked to a stop at the second floor. Robin heaved the outer door open, the elevator obviously reluctant to give up its prisoner, and stepped out of the deathtrap.

Robin could still hear the now faint voice of the little *babushka* yelling down from the ninth floor. She still couldn't understand her, but Robin guessed she was probably saying, "Lady, you should know better than to use an elevator that only works ten percent of the time. And in the future, if you get stuck, don't make so much noise."

With a newfound burst of energy, Robin bolted up the stairs to the fifth floor. She made a silent covenant with the elevator, vowing to never use it again.

17
GYPSIES
JABS
AND JARGON

"Money?" the gypsy mother said, holding out a soiled hand while supporting a sickly child on her hip. Robin just stood there dumfounded and stared.

"Sick boy," she claimed, shoving her young son in our faces. She pulled him back just long enough to hold out her hand again, rubbing her thumb back and forth across all four fingers.

The young child was covered with scabs and open sores. Patches of his hair were missing, revealing a grayish scalp. Both mother and son were filthy from head to toe, and their clothes, once bright and colorful, were now faded, torn and tattered. Though it was summer, it was still cool and damp, and the boy had no shoes.

"Do not give the gypsies anything," Alla, our guide for the day, cautioned us. "If you give them money, others will see and they will make trouble for you."

Out of pity for the boy, Robin reached into her pocket

for some *rubles*. Alla firmly grabbed Robin's arm, preventing her from pulling her hand out of her pocket.

"You must not do this," Alla insisted. "They do this
for a living. They are not poor like they want you to
believe."

Robin let go of the money, turned to Alla and said,
"But the boy is sick. Just look at him. Surely the mother
would use the money to help him. I'm sure they're hungry and they do need clothes."

"No, they are fine. Let us leave now." Alla turned to
the gypsy mother and said, *"Pashol von* [A rude way of
saying, "Get lost"]."

The mother responded with a phrase that sounded
vulgar. Mother and child immediately turned away and
headed up the hill into Red Square, searching for another gullible target.

At first, Robin refused to believe Alla's statements.
She couldn't comprehend the idea that a mother could
use her child in such a grotesque way, for profit. If it
were true, it was the most hideous form of child abuse
we had ever encountered, intentionally neglecting to
treat a child with open and oozing sores, and then pub-
licly displaying him in a scam for money. It made our
hearts sick at the time, until we had our eyes opened to
reality later in *Gum* [pronounced Goom], Moscow's
largest department store.

Gum is one of two answers to Russia's concept of a
mall. The other, *Petrovsky Passazh* [Peter's Passage], was
reserved for the wealthy. *Gum* seemed geared toward

the more common folk.

Gum's massive architecture was awesome to behold. While we were there, it was in the process of being remodeled, restored to the mint bluegreen color of years gone by. Decades of neglect had taken its toll on the structure empirically speaking. Not only could you see the fading remnants of deterioration, you could smell it as well. About one-fourth of the mall reeked with nauseating body odor. Like the resin that clings to everything long after a cigarette is gone, years of body odor clung to walls, goods and people. Through unsolicited exposure, we learned which portion of the huge department store to avoid.

While we were taking in a couple of the State-run stores in the mall, Robin sighted the gypsy mother and child huddled in a corner with a large group of gypsies. The vision left a different, but lasting, impression on us. There with the mothers and children, all looking basically the same, dirty, sickly and ragged, were husbands, dressed in nice clothes, and clean. We couldn't believe our eyes. The wives and children who had been out begging for the morning were handing over their earnings to the husbands and then heading back out on the street again for their afternoon shift. The husbands were coercing their wives into providing for them by employing fear and intimidation tactics.

"Not only do they beg for money, but if you appear frightened, they will also mug you, " Alla said, while we watched, mouths gaping. "Never let them know that you are afraid. They will take advantage of you every time."

We made a mental note of our lesson and vowed to never find ourselves in that spot. A number of our friends weren't so lucky.

One Saturday afternoon, a colleague of mine found himself at the bottom of a pile of gypsy children. Being a thin, gaunt-looking man, they figured him for an easy target. His new, white tennis shoes drew them all the more.

At first, only a couple of kids approached him asking for money. Being the gentleman that he was, he politely ignored their begging and walked on. Without warning, he found himself surrounded by twenty-five or thirty small children, all grabbing at him, trying to take anything they could get hold of. The number of kids pressing against him knocked him to the ground, signaling to the kids that they could begin untying his shoes. Not able to fight back due to a recent illness, all he could do was cry out for help. A couple of men came running, swinging wildly at the kids, not concerned that they might actually connect and send a seven-year-old flying. Once the children realized their attack was going nowhere, they disappeared as quickly as they appeared. My colleague only ended up with a few scrapes and bruises, but all the wiser for the experience.

Another colleague, much larger and with more street savvy, walked briskly into my office early one morning, out of breath and visibly shaken.

"You won't believe what just happened," he said, trembling. "You just won't believe it."

While strolling down the sidewalk on *Kutuzovsky Prospect* on his way to an early meeting, he noticed some young teenage boys trailing him. Confident that a gypsy gang wouldn't be out that early, he didn't give it a second thought, until they approached him.

The youths defiantly surrounded him, and began reaching for his briefcase and coat pockets. Like a pack of hungry wolves, while one got his attention another attempted to snatch anything he could.

My colleague, sensing that it was getting serious, pushed one of the gypsy boys out of the way and attempted to quickly move on. In retaliation, several of them pulled out large, what appeared to be hat-pins, and began threatening to make him their next pincushion.

Fearing for his life, he rushed out into the busy twelve lane street, dodging cars and buses. In hot pursuit, the youths found themselves facing off with my colleague in a temporarily unoccupied turn lane in the middle of the street.

Circling the wild-eyed businessman, each boy tried his luck at stabbing him with their five inch needles. My friend began to wonder if he was going to get any help. In a moment of miscalculation, one of the boys got smacked by a flailing briefcase, his only line of defense. The boys backed off and disappeared into the traffic empty handed.

Large hat-pins weren't the only weapons Muscovites and foreigners had to be aware of. Hypodermic syringes, with who knows what in them, had become a concern as well.

An acquaintance of ours, an American businessman working in Moscow, was injected with an unknown drug or poison while on the Metro. The attackers anticipated the businessman passing out, and their making off easily with all his possessions, but with the help of a friend the muggers failed in their efforts.

The businessman, fluent in Russian, and his partner were purchasing Metro tokens one morning. While standing in line, three Russian men approached them and began to reach for the man's briefcase and coat pockets. When he said something to them in Russian, they backed off. The two men purchased their tickets and proceeded into the Metro. The three Russians followed at a distance. Upon entering the Metro car, once again the businessman found himself facing off with the three men.

While one Russian was demanding his attention in conversation, he felt a pain in his leg. Thinking he had scraped himself on a sharp metal screw, he looked down and saw another man withdrawing a needle from his thigh. He had been injected with some unknown substance.

Terrified, the businessman and his friend got off at

the next Metro stop and headed up the stairs with the Russian robbers dogging them. Beginning to feel the effects of the injection, nausea and intense abdominal pain, his friend helped him to a nearby *kiosk* and began pleading for help. All the while, the three Russians were watching and waiting. Bent over in convulsions, unable to do anything, the businessman's friend stepped in and fended off the robbers until help came. Miraculously, the businessman survived the ordeal without losing his possessions or his health.

Whether it was gypsy children scurrying through the parks, mobbing the unsuspecting, or youth gangs running through the streets with dirty hat-pins, mugging the defenseless, or men in the Metros with syringes, everyone agreed that Moscow's crime rate was rising with alarming speed, and no one had found a lasting solution. Personal safety was the Russian citizen's primary concern.

18
SECRETARIES
SNIFFLES
AND SABOTAGE

"Hello, Rick. This is Lydia," said a familiar, faint sounding voice over the phone.

"Hi, Lydia. Are you ill again today?" I said somewhat sarcastically, forced to endure her absence time and time again.

"Yes, Rick. I am ill today," Lydia whimpered. "I believe I have food poisoning. The ambulance is coming now to pump my stomach."

"I don't think that is what you mean, Lydia. Don't you intend to go to the *Poly Clinic* and have someone treat you?"

"They will not need to take me to the *Poly Clinic*. They will pump my stomach right in my own bedroom," she said. "I have had this done before. It is not a problem."

"Okay, Lydia. Call me if you need anything." I hung up the phone, shaking my head at the ways of the

Russian medical system.

Lydia took me up on my offer. She called back at 11:00 a.m., at 1:00 p.m., at 2:30 p.m. and at 3:00 p.m., just to see how things were.

"Hello, Rick. This is Lydia."

"Hi, Lydia. What do you need this time?"

"I just wanted to say hello. I am doing better now. I think I will come to work tomorrow."

"Good. Get some rest. You don't need to worry about anything here. We've got it under control. Good-bye."

"This is good, Rick. You are such a nice man. You have done many things for me. I think I must . . . I really shouldn't . . ."

"Thank you for the compliment. I really have to be going now," I said, trying to show my sense of urgency in my voice.

"Rick, just one more thing."

"Yes, Lydia. What?"

"You know I have a dog, yes?"

"Yes, you have told me about your dog and how much you love him. It must be a very nice dog."

"He is a very good dog. He is my friend. Rick, I am worried that something may be very wrong. He has not been eating very well today. I think he is upset that I have been ill."

"Lydia, I really have to go now."

"Ah, Rick, could you do something for me?"

"What's that, Lydia?"

"Would you be so kind as to speak with my dog and cheer him up?"

"What?"

"Ah, Rick, he is a very good talker. You'll see. Let me try to get him to come to the phone."

I could hear Lydia coaxing the dog in the background. "Lydia, Lydia," I shouted. "I cannot talk to your dog over the telephone."

"This is true," she said. "He refuses to come to the phone to talk with you. Maybe he will speak with you another time. Good-bye," she said and hung up the phone.

A dark cloud seemed to follow Lydia everywhere she went. I have never known one person to encounter so much difficulty in life, and live to tell about it.

Lydia was one of five secretary/translators assigned to our office. She was in her fifties, divorced, with one son, one dog, and she was very, very lonely. And out of her quiet and desperate lifestyle, she had acquired a taste for alcohol, hoping it would become the friend she never had. Days like the dog fiasco were not at all uncommon.

For some reason, Lydia liked me. We got along great. Through the daily frustration of dealing with Russian employees in a Western style business setting, Lydia remained faithful and loyal to the end. She was the last one in our company to bid me farewell before I left for the States and then drowned her goodbyes in beer and wine. I, too, hated saying goodbye to such a trusted friend.

The dark clouds that plagued Lydia from day to day were unrelenting. Events, people, and circumstances never seemed to go in her favor.

Lydia walked into the office one morning, for example, obviously very distraught. She asked me if I had one-thousand American dollars to loan her for twenty-four hours. She had been served with papers stating that an elderly neighbor who lived next door to Lydia's son, a twenty-five year old starving musician out on his own for the first time, had decided to sue her. Lydia was being sued because she had permitted her son to become a musician and now he had become a nuisance to his community.

The son's pop-rock band regularly met in his flat for practice. Neighbors apparently didn't tolerate the noise very well, but rather than meet with the son to try to resolve the problem, they decided to go to who they thought was the source of music, Lydia. She was going to have to give an account for why she had allowed her son to pursue his dream as a musician in a band.

The neighbors wanted compensation for the inconvenience of having to listen to Lydia's son's music. I listened to their demo-tape and it really wasn't that bad, but the neighbors saw the opportunity for monetary gain, believing that being forced to listen to the music should involve some sort of payment. Since her son had no money, they went to his mother.

I didn't have the extra money to loan Lydia that day. If I did, I probably would have let her borrow it, for she always returned it as promised. Weekly, Lydia would come into the office and ask to borrow one-hundred, five-hundred or one-thousand dollars for a twenty-four hour period. If anyone in the office had it, they usually gave it to her with few questions asked. To this day, I still don't have a clue as to why she needed such large amounts of money for such short periods of time.

Lydia did settle out of court. She refused to reveal the outcome, but we all knew it involved some sort of payment.

Late one night, Lydia called me very upset over the events that had taken place that day. When she had arrived home from work that evening, an officer, with papers for another law suit, was waiting at her door. This time she was being sued for attempted murder. Another neighbor, this time her friend living directly below her, was filing the charges.

The day the restoration period hit Lydia's region of the city, it came with no announcement. As she awoke and began preparing for work, she discovered she had no water. Fully aware of the process, she immediately began boiling water for a bath. In all her preoccupation to get ready for the day, she failed to turn the hot water faucet off. One month later, disaster struck.

Just as quickly as the water was shut off, it returned. Lydia came home that evening to find her flat flooded with hot water. It had been running full-force since mid-morning. The overflow catches on the sink were not sufficient to handle the high pressure, and so it flowed over the sink onto the floor into the bedroom, into the living room, and into the kitchen of her neighbor's flat below and the neighbor's flat below that and the neighbor's flat below that. Lydia had managed to thoroughly soak four floors directly below her. The angry mob had tried to break into her flat in order to turn the water off, but the steel door wouldn't give way. Every attempt was unsuccessful. So they waited and waited.

Deeply embarrassed and apologetic, she began the task of making amends. Of course, everyone wanted money. Her neighbor immediately below her wanted a lot of money, more than Lydia was willing to pay, so the neighbor filed charges. According to the neighbor, Lydia had, in a premeditated fashion, decided that she didn't care for her and therefore had decided to murder her by drowning.

Somehow, Lydia was able to come up with enough money to satisfy her and thus avoid a trip to court. I told her that the judge would have most likely thrown the accusation of attempted murder out of court and could have acquitted her. She reminded me that all her neighbors wanted was money, and she currently had enough to satisfy their greed.

"Everything is okay now. It is not a problem," she

told me confidently.

"Ah, Rick. This is Lydia."

"You're not coming in today, right?" I said.

"Yes, Rick. I will not come in today. Perhaps I will come tomorrow."

"Okay, Lydia. Get well and we'll see you tomorrow."

"I must go to the prison today."

"Prison? What happened to you?"

"I was robbed last evening."

"Robbed? Are you okay?"

"Yes, Rick. I am okay. I was robbed by eight men. They held my dog for a two-hundred-thousand *ruble* ransom. They were going to hurt him. I tried to stop them, but they beat me up."

Lydia had been out walking her dog as the habit every evening after work. Upon returning to her building, several men came up from behind her and forced her inside. There, waiting, were a number of other men, eight in all. They surrounded Lydia and began to push her back and forth into each other's arms. One of them snatched the dog up and began to squeeze it, making it yelp. Panicked, Lydia began to cry out for mercy.

Four of the men each grabbed one of the dog's legs and began to pull in opposite directions. The dog yelped in pain. Lydia began to shout for help, but was quieted with a slap across the face, and told that if she didn't give them two-hundred-thousand *rubles*, they were going to kill the dog right there. To prove that they meant business, all four men began to once again pull the dog's legs in opposite directions, while the pet cried out in agony.

She got down on her knees and pleaded for mercy. She told them that she didn't have that kind of money. After countless minutes of trying to convince the muggers that she was telling the truth, they threw the small dog down on the concrete stairs and all eight men walked out. As they exited, each took their last shot at Lydia. Some hit her with their fist, some kicked her. She was left behind with a couple of cracked ribs, large welts on both legs, and a severely bruised face.

She was calling to let me know that some men had been arrested during the night who fit the description she gave the *Militsiya*. She had been asked to go down to the local prison and identify any who might have participated in the attack. On her way, she informed me that would she would be seeing the doctor again.

Lydia went to the *Poly Clinic* for a re-examination. While she was in the waiting room, she decided to give me a call at the office to see how things were going. While talking on the phone, someone sitting in the same room got up, nonchalantly walked over and snatched her purse, then exited the building. She didn't notice it was missing until she returned to her seat. She never recovered it.

It seemed that everything bad that could happen in a person's life did in hers. That's why with all the breaks for *chay* [tea], four or five each day, and the excessive absenteeism, I could never find it in me to dismiss her. It wouldn't have done any good to attempt to do so anyway.

There was an intriguing law, dictated during the Communist era, that had recently been upheld in the Russian court as still effectual. The law stated, in my paraphrased version, that if an individual wished to keep their job, it could never be revoked. In other words, you could have your job for as long as you lived.

The ruling came about as a result of a couple of Russian women, a mother and daughter, who brought suit against a large hotel in Moscow when they were terminated. Apparently both had been dismissed for low performance and possible theft. Some suspected them of being part of a theft-ring which organized the orderly ransacking of occupant's rooms while they were out.

Whichever the case, each woman was counseled to bring a law suit against the hotel for dismissal. Dismissal, not wrongful dismissal, was the issue. The amount sought in damages was in the millions.

After many weeks of negative publicity for both sides, it was ruled, based upon an old Communist code, that the women could have their jobs back. They were to receive full reinstatement and be paid for damages. The payment was minor compared to what they were actually seeking, but the precedent was set.

Another interesting code that Lydia adhered to closely was the law on illness in the work place. She often explained to me that during the Communist era, if anyone caught a cold, had a sniffle, or even a hint of a sniffle, they were expected to take off a couple of weeks, minimum, with all expenses paid. They were even encouraged to convalesce at the regional sanitarium [Russia's definition of a health spa]. It was enacted in order to cut down on sickness in the workplace.

In the last quarter of our stay, my driver, Yevgeny, drew upon this law when he decided to take off several weeks due to a cold and have his daughter fill in for him. Interestingly, Yevgeny expected me to pay his daughter for her time as our driver, and continue to pay him for remaining officially employed by me. I told Yevgeny that I would be more than willing to pay him if he would submit all of his earnings to the local Tax Inspectorate. He seemed to forget that old Communist law on illness.

Whether it was hourly *chay* [tea] breaks, or sniffles that would shut someone down for weeks, or jobs once created that never went away, working in Russia with any type of a work ethic was very difficult. One magazine rated Moscow as being the most difficult city in the entire world in which to do business. With only one year's exposure, I could easily see how that could be the case. It was difficult enough trying to create a Western business environment in an Eastern European Country, but it was nearly impossible to get a Russian to accept the same work ethic.

19
PRESIDENTS
PREDATORS
AND PREY

I had never had my office sniffed for bombs before, but there they were, two large German Shepherds intent on looking under every rock in the hotel, preparing for President Clinton's visit. Three floors and one elevator had been completely sealed off, reserved for the President and his staff. The large number of uniformed military personnel seemed out of place in the normally metropolitan atmosphere of the hotel.

White House staff had stayed at the hotel before. Even Vice President Gore had visited a month before, I presume laying groundwork for President Clinton's January visit. But their trips were minor compared to the attention that President Clinton's stay commanded.

Things were definitely going to be different that week. New Chevrolet® Suburbans, normally a rare sight in Moscow, now surrounded the hotel. Barricades were set up, preventing the taxi mafia from claiming their reg-

ular turf on the hotel grounds. Hotel and business center staff were all abuzz, swapping tales of previous
encounters with important people. The media continually speculated on why the President had decided to
stay at the hotel and not at the Embassy House.

The business center side of the hotel had been singled
out as a mecca of communications for Eastern Europe.
Reuters, ABC, the International Press Club, and numerous foreign television stations had already leased space
in the business center long before President Clinton's
visit. One of my assigned projects was to assist one of
our architects in managing the construction of a television studio on the hotel roof, making things fairly convenient for CNN and the major American networks who
followed Clinton around the world to temporarily set-
up shop. A number of well-known news celebrities had
leased office space as well, so I was often surprised by
who I met on the elevator.

A colleague of mine had been a former employee of
the American Embassy in Moscow for a number of
years. He had been heavily involved in coordinating
President Bush's visit several years earlier. It was fascinating to hear him describe all the preparation for a
Presidential visit, the communications links, the security, and all the publicity.

Our office was located on the fifth floor of the hotel
which overlooked a small portion of the circular drive.
By coincidence, it was that small portion of the drive
where President Clinton's limousine parked, just off the

main drive, so we found ourselves peering out the office window hourly seeing if we could catch a glimpse of the President. We saw the Suburbans, we saw the limousines, we saw the Secret Service, but we never saw the President, and I think they wanted it that way.

Being up on the fifth floor did provide us with some entertainment during that time. Getting into the business elevator the first morning of the President's stay, I noticed a man following me. He was dressed in black, wearing what appeared to be black motocross boots, and toting a black canvas bag. He was athletic, intent, and seemed very saturnine. He got out on the third floor, while I continued to the fifth.

A couple of my colleagues were already peering out the window, having heard word that the President was getting ready to leave the hotel for a meeting with President Yeltsin. Looking down on the complex, we could easily see the second floor roof jutting out from the main building, housing the large skylight for the business center. This second floor roof protruded right over the door where President Clinton entered and exited.

That same man I saw in the elevator was positioned on the second floor roof directly overlooking the door. He was wearing a black ski mask and was assembling an automatic weapon with a large scope with perfunctory ease. He pulled a couple of other unidentified things out of his bag and laid them in the snow beside him. This professional was strategically placed to ensure the

President's safety against any sniper attacks. He looked to be Russian, but I didn't know for sure. We could only guess as to how many other such men were placed in, on, and around the building.

With camera in hand, my co-worker began to snap a few pictures of the man in black. Looking bored, the man began to train his automatic weapon on different objects surrounding the building. A large bird flew directly over his head. He followed its every move with his scope. Trailing the bird's flight pattern forced him to turn one-hundred and eighty degrees away from his assignment. It was a picture an employee hoped their boss would never see.

A few minutes later, the man redirected his attention to his duties, the President exited the building, and sped off in his cavalcade. The masked man disappeared off the roof, only to return a couple of hours later when the President returned. Luckily, no more birds flew over.

On a Friday night, the last night of President Clinton's stay in Moscow, I experienced one of the most embarrassing moments of my life.

Friday morning, the papers informed us that President Yeltsin had personally invited President Clinton and his wife and daughter to spend Friday night, the last night of their stay, in the Kremlin. It was the first time any U.S. President had received the invitation. President Clinton decided to accept the gracious offer.

Weary of all the extra security at the hotel, and all the hoopla surrounding the visit, I was glad for Friday evening to arrive, knowing President Clinton was probably already at the Kremlin eating caviar and chilled sturgeon. Walking out of my office at 6:00 p.m. sharp, I decided I would stop by my friend's office on the third floor and wish him and his family a good weekend.

Having already gone for the day, his office was locked tight. I decided rather than walk back all the way around the building to the business center elevator, I would take the main hotel elevators. *They are right there and President Clinton was gone,* or so I thought.

I pushed the elevator button and waited. Elevator number one rang and the doors opened. It was the elevator that had been reserved for President Clinton, but I assumed they would have secured it to travel just between his floor and the lobby if he were still there. I stepped in, pushed the button for the first floor, and waited.

The first floor chimed and the doors opened. Standing there with bright lights shining behind him, emulating a halo around his head, was Dan Rather. He was smiling, apparently ready to greet the President. He looked me over, wiped the smile from his face and replaced it with a scowl. Dropping his microphone to his side, he took a couple of steps back and glared at me in disdain.

I stood in the large vacant lobby with just Dan Rather

and his cameraman. Hundreds of people were standing behind the large set of glass doors, now sealed off by the Secret Service. I noticed our General Director standing behind the Lobby Desk, mouth gaping in disbelief.

Trying to gain my composure, I sashayed up to the desk. "What's going on?" I said, ears burning with embarrassment.

"The President is coming out any minute now. If you were going to leave, this would be a good time to do so."

I walked toward the glass doors, the crowd staring intently at me as if I were a part of the event, and I allowed the Secret Service person to open the door for me. She put her hand in the middle of my back and pressed me out into the crowd. The door closed behind me just as President Clinton walked in.

Once again, there was Dan Rather in the bright lights with smile and handshake in place.

"Excuse me, please. Ah, excuse me."

Someone was trying to make their way through the crowd. To my surprise, it was the Secretary of State and the Secretary of the Treasury. Both were entering through the front door, out of the bright light, forced to fight with the crowd with minimal assistance.

As they walked right past me, I was tempted to lean over and whisper, "Hey, don't feel badly. It's no picnic being in the bright lights." But somehow, I don't think they would have understood.

20
BUSINESS BARBECUES AND BAD GUYS

"You must come to my boyfriend's *dacha* [country home] for a Sunday afternoon," Katia pleaded. "He is a very nice man. He has a large house in the country and the food will be very good."

It didn't take a lot to convince us that a day out of Moscow would be a welcome reprieve from the three months of cabin fever. We gladly accepted the offer and decided that a sunny Sunday afternoon in June would be best. Andrei, our driver, talked with Katia and agreed on a rendezvous spot where we would meet her and her boyfriend and follow them out to his *dacha*.

With several new Western housing developments underway, there are a few, though still unaffordable, single family houses in Moscow. Most Russians, if given the choice, prefer to own a *dacha* reserved for vacations and weekends and live in a flat during the week. Most *dachas* were without running water and electricity, so the trips to the country were limited to late spring, summer and early fall. Typical *dachas* were meager dwellings, made out of whatever was available at the time of construction. Primitive would be the best description, but that wasn't the case with Katia's boyfriend's *dacha*.

Right after church we rushed across town to meet our hosts. Running a few minutes late, I figured that we would actually be on time according to Moscow standards. Normally very punctual, I wasn't too concerned that particular Sunday, it was a day set aside for relaxation, no clocks, no appointments, no hassles. We were going to take full advantage and soak up the Russian countryside.

"Look at that," I exclaimed.

Parked on the side of the road at a small intersection was a new, bright red Dodge® Stealth.

"I wonder who owns that?" I said, openly admiring the sleek look. In the fleet of *Volgas* and *Ladas* that crowded the city streets, it was a rare sight in Moscow. I wanted to make the moment last.

"This is your friend's boyfriend," Andrei informed me. "She told me that he had a red sports car."

We were actually going to have lunch with a Dodge Stealth. At least we would be in the same vicinity. Sure enough, there was Katia, sitting in the passenger seat. We did a quick U-turn and pulled up behind them. Andrei stepped out and informed them we were ready. The Dodge Stealth pulled out, throwing dirt and pebbles up into the air, leaving us behind in a cloud. Andrei was up to the challenge and pushed his little Nissan as hard as it would go, until everyone slowed down when we reached the outskirts of town.

The trees, a luscious deep, dark green outlined with white bark, offered a refreshing respite from the pollution of the city. We were determined to enjoy the trip.

We followed the red blur through the winding country road for about ten miles. Finally, he slowed long enough to make a right turn into a drive leading into a large compound. Barricaded by huge, ominous looking iron gates, three armed men in military fatigues stepped into the pathway of the Stealth and halted it. After a couple minutes of what appeared to be light conversation, one of the men opened the gates and waved both cars on through. As we slowly passed by the guards, they meticulously looked us over.

Through those gates we entered another world. As we drove down the unusually manicured, tree lined street, we were awestruck at the large homes neatly tucked away several hundred feet off the beaten path, each well-groomed and alluring in its own unique way. Driveways harbored two or three late model cars. Jeeps, Mercedes, Volvos, BMWs, and mini-vans seemed to be the most common modes of transportation. For a brief moment, I thought I was in Aspen.

It was a community devoted to, and laid aside for, the rich. They were the Russian elite that the common people heard about, but never get a chance to see, except perhaps through a tinted car window. And we were going to have lunch with them.

After a few hundred yards of seemingly driving six inches off the ground, we came to a halt in a driveway of a large, three-story home with an oversized two-car garage. In front of the garage stood a huge white dog chained to a tree.

The kids jumped out of the car and sprinted up to Katia, embracing her with hugs and kisses. They immediately began asking her if they could pet the dog. Unfortunately, the dog had been trained for protection, so the kids were out of luck. In fact, they were warned to not go near the dog.

Katia's boyfriend surprised me. Being a successful and attractive model herself, I had expected someone striking, like a Ken doll. He was young, but very average looking. Although sharply dressed, his clothes didn't conceal his spare tire. He was different from who I had envisioned.

"Come, let me introduce you to my boyfriend and his friends," Katia said, smiling graciously. We shook hands with her boyfriend, who then quickly excused himself and disappeared with a group of men around the corner. We were introduced to a number of different people who were scurrying about, busily preparing a huge meal to be eaten outdoors on the long, but elegant, picnic table.

We didn't see the boyfriend again until dinner time. I don't think he was intentionally avoiding us, he just seemed preoccupied with giving all his associates rides in his car.

Andrei reacted very strangely to the whole ordeal. He refused to get out of his car, assuring us he would be fine and could use the extra time to work on his electrical wiring. Trusting his assessment of situations, we wished he had gotten more involved.

The kids were given the run of the place, upstairs, downstairs, indoors, and outdoors. Katia took them for a long walk down a garden path, looking for things of interest. Barring the swarms of mosquitoes, it was truly a haven of rest.

We sat down to a feast of fresh garden salads, potatoes, barbecued meats, wine, vodka, champagne, and more desserts than we could possibly eat. The table was packed with friends and family, about twenty in all.

It was my opportunity to converse with Katia's boyfriend. In between answering his cellular phone, and disappearing around the corner, speaking with men who refused to come to the table, I was able to ask him what he did for a living. Speaking no English, he told Katia to tell me that he was in, *"Beezniz."*

"What type of business are you in?" I said. Robin nudged me lightly under the table.

"Oil, transactions, a little of this, a little of that," he replied through Katia.

"You are so young for such success," I continued. "What is the name of your business?" This time Robin let me have it under the table.

"It is not important. I am in *Beezniz*," he replied once

again through Katia.

After another kick under the table, I changed the subject. I asked him how he liked his car. He told me he enjoyed it so much he had decided to order the newer model the last time he was in New York City and was preparing to have it shipped over. While he was describing his buying escapades, I was constantly sizing him up, still wondering how a twenty-eight-year-old could find so much wealth so quickly.

We were asked to share our impressions of Moscow and Russia. We talked of both the good and the difficult. Fresh on our minds, we shared our recent situation with the theft of all my summer shirts. Upon hearing the story, Katia's boyfriend disappeared inside the house and quickly returned with a dress shirt, still in its package. He told Katia that he would like to make the shirt a gift, a token of friendship. He also told me he identified with the difficulty of finding nice XL and XXL shirts in Russia, so he chose to purchase his wardrobe in Italy. I thanked him profusely for his generosity.

Sensing my persistence for steering the conversation back to his business ventures, Robin frantically fended me off by redirecting our attention to the children. A silver-haired man sitting next to me seemed fascinated with Seth and his command of English. Genuinely interested in our visit, we struck up a conversation, through Katia, about his line of work. Receiving no kicks under the table, I asked about his background.

Trained in Russia as an Oncologist, he seemed to

speak with contempt for his profession. Impressed with his credentials and the ease with which I was able to carry on a conversation with him even with the disadvantage of a translator, I attempted to discuss with him the obvious need for new medical technology for the common people. He informed me that he just recently had stepped out of the profession and was not interested in going back into it anytime soon.

"I did not make money as a doctor," he said with a grimace. "I make much more money here on weekends working as a cook for my friend. Besides, I enjoy this work. Do you like my food?"

The food was wonderful and the hospitality strangely magnetic. After a number of toasts, we sat back, ready to go into another food coma. Katia offered to take the four of us for a walk around the lake. The kids jumped at the idea. Katia's boyfriend disappeared again around the corner, busy with friends and associates coming and going all afternoon.

Walking down toward the lake, Robin pulled me off to the side and began to quietly scold me. "What did you think you were doing asking him all those questions?" she snapped. "Haven't you caught on as to what he does for a living?"

"What are you talking about?" I said.

"Can we say, organized crime? Corruption? Illegal business?"

It all made sense to me then. And I had been hurling questions at him that he was uncomfortable answering.

Katia walked up and said, "You know, Rick, it is probably best not to ask him about his business."

"Do you talk to him about it?" I said.

"No, he has asked me not to discuss his business. I am his girlfriend, not his associate."

Our walk around the lake was a welcome distraction from the current events. There were several fishermen with cane poles in hands, sitting on the bank, waiting. One man actually had several medium-sized fish on a stringer.

"Can you eat the fish you catch?" Seth said.

"Perhaps, but it is better that we feed them to our cats," the man said.

After our walk around the lake, we found ourselves seated once again at the table discussing customs and traditions of both countries. This time two attractive young girls arrived, stayed for a bit, and then disappeared.

"Do people come and go all the time?" I said, careful not to push for too much information.

"Yes, it is like this every Sunday. In fact, we would like to invite you to come again next Sunday. He has told me that his house is your house. You will come, yes?" Katia said.

"We will have to wait and see," I said, glancing over at Robin, wondering if she were beginning to feel as uncomfortable as I, fearful that we might be raided by the good guys or the bad guys at any moment.

Several men gathered around a makeshift campfire

and began roasting fish, eating it right off the bone. Everyone appeared to enjoy it, but Robin and I politely refused the invitation to partake. We were still digesting the huge meal we had eaten only a couple of hours ago.

As we said our goodbyes, the kids were showered with Russian candy. The former Oncologist insisted that I come back and visit him next weekend. He told Katia that he enjoyed getting to know me and hoped I would return to taste his food again very soon. Katia's boyfriend said his goodbye, offered the use of his house anytime, and then disappeared. We headed back to the car, finding Andrei engrossed in the side panel of his door. Wiring was everywhere but he was relieved to see us and put everything back together with remarkable speed.

Our journey back to the city was charged with the current attention being given to organized crime in Moscow. Andrei knew what Katia's boyfriend did for a living the second he saw him. It came as no surprise. He began to tell us stories, kept to himself until then, of the widespread corruption in the Moscow business world. I resolved not to find myself in that situation again, completely naive.

Whether you are Russian or American, native or foreigner, doing business in Russia can be very risky. Many compare Moscow to Capone's Chicago. It was no surprise that crime and corruption were the number one action item on the Russian agenda.

Whether it be thugs, unwilling to wait for the green light, driving their Mercedes down crowded sidewalks, sending pedestrians scurrying for cover, or bullies pushing their way to the front of a long queue, daring anyone to say challenge them, corruption was alive and flourishing in Russia.

It was a society with two dominant classes, the rich and the poor. Although a middle-class structure was attempting to carve out a niche for themselves, I believe it will be years before that group significantly impacts the already imbalanced society.

Business in Russia definitely had its pros and cons. If you were an entrepreneur and you had good business sense, it could be a land of opportunity. If you were financially successful at what you did, had a high profile, and were in business for any length of time, you could bet that another opportunity would come knocking as well. You would be privileged to hand over protection money and possibly a portion of your ownership, in order to keep your business prosperous.

If people refused, they might receive a hand-grenade while eating their lunch, or have automatic weapons riddling their flat. A bomb might destroy their business, or they could be kidnaped and held for ransom.

Literally hundreds of foreign businessmen, looking for financial gain and independence in Russia, have been prematurely sent to the grave instead, snuffed out because they were effective businessmen. These men and women serve as vivid memorials, tragic reminders that living in Moscow was not something to be taken lightly.

Many Russians believe that the person in the greatest danger was the Russian partner in any joint-venture company. They believe that the Russian partner could be easily compromised for both good and bad influences, and was the one in the partnership least likely to attract an intense investigation. That way the killers were less likely to be apprehended and could still get their point across. That may be changing as organized crime in Russia becomes more and more bold in its criminal acts against foreigners.

Another trend in Moscow was the Russian partner's aggressive attempt to repossess the joint-venture business once firmly established. The pattern had been to entice the foreigners interested in making money, exploit their management expertise, make the business profitable, then force the foreigners out. Recent government policies and a heavy hand have given these Russians enough legal ammunition to successfully pull this off in several large joint-ventures.

There was no business, no matter how large or small, immune to the criminal influence in Russia. Where there was a lot of money to be made, there would be those who attempted to take it by force. The bank president sitting behind his walnut desk, secure in his office and the kiosk owner sitting on his bar stool in his converted shed are equally susceptible to the same violence and corruption.

Even Robin was offered several lucrative opportunities to start a baking business, providing American-style cookies, pastries and pies. Robin could have made a lot of money in a very short period of time. But we didn't want the hassle of being forced to do business with those we preferred to avoid.

It was a typical summer Sunday afternoon in Moscow. Most of the city had left, seeking greener pastures at their *dachas,* leaving the streets barren, when, looking for something to do, a friend of mine opened her hotel room drapes to get a view of the Moscow River below. Although polluted from barges and factories, it still offered a somewhat pleasant picture with European taste.

While watching people and cars just across the River on *Rostovskaya naberezhnaya,* she saw a *Volga* swerve in between two barricades, recently placed there temporarily as a result of a car being dumped in the River, narrowly miss each of them, and drive right off into the River.

She couldn't believe her eyes. There were three men in the car as it began to sink. Everything disappeared. She froze, not knowing what to do, and just watched and waited for any signs of life.

Moments later, she saw three heads pop up out of the water and begin to make their way to shore. Already, several cars had stopped and a crowd was beginning to gather. Bubbles continued to spew from where the car was last seen.

The three men made it safely to the bank and climbed up the long makeshift rope, perhaps placed there for similar situations. After reaching the top of the concrete embankment, one of the three men ran off, disappearing into the trees across the street.

A *GAI* [traffic cop] pulled up, got out and began talking to the two remaining men. After a few minutes of discourse, unannounced, one of the two men stripped down to his skivvies, in front of everyone, and dove back into the River, swimming back out to where the car had gone down. With a deep breath, he disappeared. After what seemed to be minutes, he reappeared and made his way back to the rope. This time he had something in his hand. It was his sports coat.

He climbed back up the rope, redressed as if nothing had happened, and put on his soaked sports coat. Both men talked with the *GAI* a few more minutes, then disappeared down the street.

It is anyone's guess how many cars sit at the bottom of the Moscow River, though a number of them were retrieved and made the headlines in the local newspapers. While in Moscow, it wasn't uncommon to read on the front page of the Moscow Times about a BMW or Mercedes being hauled out of the River. When owners were asked why their cars had ended up in the River, more often than not their response was, *"Beezniz."*

21
COUPS
COMRADES
AND KIDS

It was Sunday, October 3. Andrei, and I had wagered when the first snowfall would hit Moscow. I had predicted Halloween, while Andrei had predicted the first weekend of October. He won. The white dusting began to mentally prepare us for the harsh Russian winter that lie ahead.

"I think you will not be going to Church today," Andrei said as we drove up to Lenin's Square. "This does not look good."

The entire Square was surrounded with government troops standing at attention, shoulder to shoulder, fully decked out in their riot gear. Several large water cannons, armored personnel carriers, and sizeable artillery pieces stood silent, ready to offer backup if called upon.

"Ask someone what is going on," I instructed Andrei, as we coasted cautiously around the Square, pulling up to Lenin's Children's Library where the Church was meeting.

Andrei jumped out of the car, trotted over to an officer who appeared to be in charge, and inquired about
the situation. We climbed out of the car, seeking to get a
better look at all the commotion. It was all I could do to
contain Seth, mesmerized with the weaponry, now
within easy reach.

Being members of the Church's contemporary worship team, we had arrived early for band practice, but
we didn't expect to be the first ones. Even the Library,
normally open by that time, was locked tight. We had
heard a rumor about a demonstration, but it looked like
it was going to be much more than that.

A few minutes later, our Pastor's family drove up,
just as surprised as we were. Unsure what our next
move should be, we all stood around staring at one
another. We decided we would wait for Andrei to
return before making any decisions.

"It is going to be bad, Rick," Andrei said, out of
breath from his brisk walk across the Square. "Today is
going to be a very large demonstration of hardline
Communists. I think they may do some crazy things."

"What do we do?"

"The officer told me that we may stay until twelve-
thirty p.m., but after that, barricades will go up and we
will not be able to exit the Square with my car. The
demonstration will begin at two p.m."

After of a couple of minutes of intensive evaluation,
we decided to go ahead and hold the worship service in

the Library. Using our Pastor's persuasive powers, we convinced the Director of the Library to open the doors after reassuring her that we would vacate by 12:15 p.m. Andrei, fearful that his car might be a target for early arrivals, decided to stand guard over it, and agreed to let us know if something serious developed.

We sang, we read the Bible, we worshiped, we prayed, while pondering what we could be facing outside. After worship, we were instructed to leave the Square immediately. The worship band scurried about, putting away their instruments and the sound system in record time. We walked out of the Library at 12:15 p.m. There, feeling the tension in the air, Andrei had his car doors open, anxiously awaiting our return.

"Let us go quickly," Andrei said, grabbing the bass guitar out of my hand and tossing it in the trunk.

Looking out over the Square, it appeared that nothing had changed over the last two hours. I thought maybe the demonstrators found out about the government forces and decided to retreat.

The May Day riot, initiated in Lenin's Square and quickly spilling out into *Leninsky Prospect*, was still fresh on everyone's mind. Several vehicles had been destroyed and a number of people seriously injured. No one had anticipated that the hardliners would become violent during their demonstration -- hardliners were defined as those who opposed democracy and sought to restore Communism -- but the troops would be ready for them this time.

A friend once told me, "Accidents are miracles of timing." I'm sure some would consider our showing up for Church on Sunday, October 3, an accident. If that were the case, then our timing was perfect.

We drove out of the Square at exactly 12:20 p.m. Ten minutes later, at 12:30 p.m., several thousand hardline demonstrators showed up an hour and half early, voicing their support of the hardline Parliamentarians, currently holed up in the White House in defiance of President Yeltsin's orders to vacate.

Slowly passing by *Gorky Park,* just down the street from Lenin's Square, we got the definite impression that something big was about to happen. At the entrance to the Park, a crowd had gathered, many of them waving the bright red Communist flag with the yellow hammer and sickle. Several had bullhorns, shouting Communist slogans and democratic slurs. We drove home in silence, praying that things would not get too far out of hand.

The telephone rang. It was a close friend of ours, concerned about our welfare.

"Rick, are you guys okay?"

"Sure, why do you ask?" I said.

"You aren't listening to the radio?"

"You know I don't understand Russian," I said. "And it isn't time for the English speaking news."

"The hardliners have attempted to start a coup. It

started at the rally in Lenin's Square this afternoon. Ten thousand Communists have gone to the White House in support of Rutskoi. They have overrun the Mayor's office and now they've been ordered to take the Communications Tower. They're heading toward *Ostankino* [the Television Communication Station and Tower]."

Our friend lived in a Westernized flat overlooking the Garden Ring Road, directly in the path leading from the White House to *Ostankino*. Born in Russia and educated in New Jersey, he was fluent in both Russian and English. He had been listening to the English speaking news on a local FM station and watching Russian television, trying to make sense of what was going on.

"Are you okay?" I asked.

"Sure, but it's pretty bizarre. I'm looking out my window right now. Thousands of people are walking up the middle of the street, stopping all traffic, smashing car windows and trying to steal anything they can. I don't think calling the *Militsiya* is going to do any good. I have a sneaking suspicion they are already aware of it anyway. I saw a couple of guys trying to hot-wire a truck parked in front of my flat with no one trying to stop them. I thought about yelling down at them from the window, but I don't want a bunch of rioters running up the stairs mad at me."

"Thanks for calling. I'll listen to the radio. If you hear anything on Russian television you think we need to know, please call." We said goodbye, promising to remain in close contact.

The radio station was abuzz with news of the alleged takeover of the Mayor's office. Reports were sketchy, but it appeared that the Parliamentarians had rallied the hardliners to start taking back what was once theirs. At last report, they were heading toward *Ostankino*. Strategically speaking, it was believed that whoever had control of communications in Moscow would have the edge in the escalating civil war.

We were being told to remain indoors and stay tuned to the radio station for further developments. An Embassy alert had gone out to all ex-pats warning foreigners that, due to the current Civil unrest, they should avoid large crowds and gatherings. Evacuation procedures were put in place, to be followed exactly if the orders were given.

I speculated how we would get to the airport, or the Embassy if required. Having no transportation, we would be forced to take the public Metro, risking bringing attention to ourselves and possible harm. Being the only Americans for blocks and discovering that every Russian in the neighborhood knew where we lived, I prayed there weren't any disgruntled *Muscovites* tempted to take their frustrations out on us.

The telephone rang. It was Andrei.

"Rick, I do not think you will go to work tomorrow," Andrei said, mixing sarcasm with tension and uneasiness.

"What do you mean?"

"It is like Afghanistan near my house. I hear lots of guns and explosions. I think the Communists are trying to take *Ostankino.* It is crazy, a Civil War in my own city. I think these hardliners want to make everything as it was, but I think Yeltsin's men will not let them."

I asked Andrei if he and his family would be okay. He was certain they would and assured me that we had nothing to worry about as long as we remained inside. I couldn't help wondering if he was hiding his apprehension behind his stoic Russian manner.

We turned the Russian television on, hoping we could interpret the reports, or if we were lucky, catch an English speaking news bulletin. We found one channel reporting on the uprising. As they were showing video clips of angry mobs, suddenly the television screen turned to snow. We switched channels and found the same thing. The signal had been cut off.

Switching to an FM radio station, offering updates every five minutes or so, we found ourselves hanging on every word. In between reports we called our family in the States. They were greatly relieved to hear from us, having already received footage on the uprising over their local TV stations. After saying our goodbyes and expressing our longing to be safe at home in the States, we decided there was nothing else we could do, and went to bed. The last thing I remember before falling asleep was hearing the announcement that the hardliners had been unsuccessful in their first attempt to take *Ostankino*. The brief confrontation in north Moscow turned out to be the bloodiest conflict of the rebellion, costing many innocent lives.

Later we found out how close the hardliners had come to actually changing the outcome of the battle at *Ostankino*. It was reported that Yeltsin's forces had arrived only thirty seconds ahead of the hardliners. As they entered the building, they had less than a minute to turn about face, load their weapons and prepare to meet their foes. That thirty seconds could have changed the bulletins broadcasted to the Russian population, the brief civil war could have had a drastically different outcome.

"Hey, this is Rick," surprised to find my co-worker in the office, "How are things at the business center?"

"I don't think you will want to come into work today," he said. "Listen to this." He opened the window, allowing the sound of large artillery and automatic weapon fire to fill the room, and the phone.

"I think everything's busted loose," he said. "Yeltsin's not going to stand for this stuff any more. He wants 'em out of there. They've got tanks on *Kalininsky* Bridge, military helicopters circling the place and I don't think they're going anywhere soon."

"Let me know if you hear anything new," I said. "Are you going to be okay?"

"Don't worry about me, I'll just do some work in the office and if I get bored I'll walk over to my flat and have a caviar sandwich and a beer and watch the fireworks from there." A seasoned ex-pat having worked overseas for years, events like this had little effect on him.

We listened to the radio and kept an eye on the restored Russian television signal throughout the day. Detailed accounts were given describing the pounding Yeltsin's troops were giving the hardliners. Earlier that morning, just as we opened our own windows, we heard a distant tank blast. Even though we lived several miles from the conflict, we could discern periodic explosions of the larger caliber weapons. Stories came across the wire of secret tunnels the hardliners were using to get in and out of the White House.

As the conflict spread, rumors of sniper fire from rooftops on *Novy Arbat* were confirmed as the wounded began to fill hospitals. Frozen in their tracks, refusing to believe what was happening in their city, innocent bystanders became easy targets for the indiscriminate hardliners.

As the day wore on and the troops continued their assault on the White House, it became apparent that the hardliners were going to be soundly defeated. At dusk, the two leaders of the uprising, Khasbulatov and Rutskoi were lead out of the White House, officially surrendering to Yeltsin. The conflict was over for most people.

A few of those who had managed to evade the siege

vowed that the conflict, largely confined on October 4 to the grounds immediately surrounding the White House, would evolve into urban guerrilla warfare.

The following morning the radio station suggested once again that all foreigners remain inside for at least one more day. Random sniper fire had been reported in populous spots around the city. Some locations mentioned were close to our flat.

When I decided I would go to work on Tuesday, Robin was understandably concerned I might be the target of violence and pleaded with me to reconsider. With the White House being just four blocks away from my office, I wanted to see firsthand what the reporters had been describing.

After convincing Robin I needed to get back to work, we decided it would be okay for Seth to go back to school as well. Since it was on the outskirts of Moscow, in the opposite direction of the conflict, we figured he would be safe. But first, Andrei would have to take me to work.

Since we were already in the car, the White House only a couple of blocks away, and with the road leading by my office also leading right by the White House, I asked Andrei to drive by.

Seth was taken back at the sight. I don't think he expected all the damage. As we drove closer to the blackened building he said, "Daddy, did tanks do all that?"

"They did a lot of it," I said.

As Seth moved closer to the window his eyes grew large. "Daddy, look. They even broke out all the windows."

Even with the rumors of sniper fire still around the White House, I had Andrei stop the car. I took a chance, jumped out and asked him to take a quick picture with the charred building in the background.

When I arrived at work everyone had their own version of the conflict to embellish. Bullets had been found on the rooftop of our building and in the garden in front of the hotel. Some of my colleagues had been trapped in their flat, right around the corner from the White House. They witnessed an innocent bystander shot as they peeked out their window. Paralyzed by the gunfire, they could do nothing except watch him lie there, bleeding.

Looking out our windows toward the White House that Monday, we took our life into our own hands. A young family member of a couple we knew tragically perished at the hands of a stray bullet. While standing innocently in the picture window of his parent's flat, gazing down upon the catastrophe, a sniper's bullet found his chest. Death and destruction personally touched many who we knew.

One of my colleagues and a friend had spent most of Sunday night at the White House behind enemy lines just quietly observing with video and 35-mm cameras. Hour after hour, they watched the Communists build numerous barricades out of anything that wasn't bolted down. Men moved the heavy stuff, while the women pitched in and helped stretch barbed wire. All night long, through the ear shattering noise blaring from the loudspeakers and the blinding spotlights trained on the building, they silently labored, preparing to make their stand.

The next day my colleague and his friend ventured out once again into the line of fire. Like tornado chasers, they were intent on experiencing the thrill of danger. With the first tank blast to hit the White House, they knew it was going to get bloody. They witnessed a sniper taken out of a top floor, numerous hardliners captured and taken prisoner throughout the day, and former KGB agents, now Yeltsin supporters, pinned down and returning fire.

Crouched down out of sight, or so they thought, bullets struck the surrounding trees and bushes as hardliners began shooting at them. A soldier in a bulletproof vest came to their rescue, stepping out into the street retaliating with heavy weapon fire, offering precious seconds for my colleague and his friend to safely escape.

I was fortunate enough to get a copy of the video and some gripping snapshots of the conflict in action. Every time I am tempted to complain of my present circumstances, I pull out the video and recall once again what the Russian people were forced to endure.

The White House, a blackened shell, served a testimonial to two distinct philosophies unable to coexist, completely incompatible with each other. Understandably uncomfortable with the entire incident, President Yeltsin immediately engaged a company to restore the White House to its original condition with breakneck speed. Within days, a huge green tarp draped the front of the White House, forever concealing the remains of the rebellion.

A week later, after Church, we took a drive down *Novy Arbat* and the Ring Road to see the aftermath of twisted steel, burned out cars and splintered barricades, allowing war to have its full impact on us.

"Mommy, does President Yeltsin have kids?" Seth asked.

"Yes, I believe he does," Robin said.

"Does he go on vacations?"

"I'm sure he does when he has the time."

"Does he take his kids with him?"

"I would think so," she answered.

"Do you think he's happy right now?" he said, staring out the window.

"I don't know, he's gone through a lot in the last few weeks. There are a lot of people who want someone else to be President," Robin said.

"Do you think he's tired of all the fighting?"

"Probably so, sweetie," Robin said giving him a hug. "Why do you ask?"

"I think I would like to ask President Yeltsin if he would like to come over to my house to play," Seth said.

"Why would you like to do that?" I said, glancing over my shoulder.

"I would like to ask him to come over to my house and play because I think he needs to get away from all those mean people. If he does come over, we wouldn't play with my tank or my guns. We would play with nice things, because, I think he needs a rest."

"I think you're probably right," Robin said, reaching over and stroking his head gently. "I think you're probably right."

22
LAUGHTER
LEGENDS
AND LAMENTS

"It is not a problem, Rick. He wanted two-thousand *rubles.* I told him I should not give him so much money for such a crazy fine. He agreed and asked for five-hundred *rubles.* I paid him. It is not a problem. Let's go."

Andrei, our driver, had just been stopped by a *GAI* [traffic cop]. We waited inside the car while Andrei negotiated with the officer in his tiny makeshift shelter just off the road. It was close enough to the intersection to observe oncoming traffic, but far enough off the road to be safe should a drunken motorist mistake the sidewalk for a road.

"It is a crazy city," Andrei said. "He wanted two-thousand *rubles* because my car was dirty. I told him why I could not wash it today. I told him that I had to take foreigners to an appointment and that I was in a big hurry. He insisted I give him something. If I did not, he might do something crazy, like take my license plate away from me until I pay the fine. I think he must buy his wife something special tonight."

Once every two or three weeks, Andrei was sure to be stopped by the *GAI*, usually for something ludicrous. Every time we passed by one, I prayed he would not recognize us, waving his white baton at our car, directing us over to the curb. *GAI* seemed to loom at every intersection, waiting to pounce on their next victim. I noticed they seemed to stop older Russian-made cars more often than foreign imports, but I don't know why.

Corruption in Moscow was not limited to criminals behind tinted windows. A traffic cop on the corner, receiving a scant municipal salary, could be just as venal as the unethical businessman racing by him in a BMW. Though he may not make as much money in one day as the crook in the car, with a little persistence, he could walk away with a substantial amount of cash at the end of his shift. Thankfully, not all traffic cops were that way. We met a few *GAI* who were professional and courteous in the discharge of their duty. They executed their job with pride. I appreciated these professionals being there even when my driver was fined for neglecting a traffic ordinance.

I wish we had met more *GAI* like this, but unfortunately, many of the *GAI* who waved us over were not pillars of ethical values. A dirty car, a dented fender, a missing hubcap, or a door primered in a different color were often sufficient reason to pull one over and demand *rubles*. Andrei rarely tolerated the hassle. If he sensed the *GAI* was crooked, he would threaten to go on down to the precinct and take up the issue with his superior. That often squelched the demand. Still, precious minutes were wasted every time one waved you over to the side of the road.

On several occasions Andrei convinced the *GAI* that he had very important foreign diplomats in the car. At first, we couldn't figure out why the officer would approach the car, lean over and peer in at us. Andrei hated the rampant corruption, but refused to admit that he shouldn't fight corruption with corruption.

Andrei taught us a lot about the streets of Moscow, when he slowed down long enough to have a conversation. He showed us how to tell what business a person was in and where they were from by the license plate on their car. He pointed out the first three letters on license plates which labeled the former KGB. According to many Russians, the three most common combinations identifying the KGB were *ММГ, ММБ,* and *ММЖ.*

As a regular passenger at the mercy of the Moscow streets, I only wished there were more road crews assigned to street repair. As it was, the only crews we ever saw patching up the constantly crumbling asphalt were women who appeared to be fifty years and older. I saw so many of them, I began to wonder if older, seasoned, and more mature females fit the job description for road crews.

One day while waiting for a green light, I recall watching a crew work right next to us. Some of the women scooped the warm asphalt out of the back of a truck and scattered it with their shovels, other women packed it down with whatever was handy that day, including their boots. Sitting in the cab manning the truck was the only male figure present on the crew.

For several weeks we did see one large road crew actually resurfacing a small section of road with a large resurfacer and huge heavy steamrollers. All involved in that project were men. I don't know if the city was intending to send a message to those observing the work being done, but they did. Women seemed to land the physically demanding grunt jobs while men got to play on all the big machines.

The streets were not only in disarray aesthetically speaking, but they were dangerous as well. I recall two instances where people lost their lives due to the neglect of regular maintenance on the city's infrastructure.

Two city workers assigned to inspect and repair a small portion of the centralized hot water system found themselves under the scrutiny of city officials for criminal acts of negligence. Working near an elementary school, the employees had temporarily removed a manhole cover in order to do their work. Walking off the job to take a break, they failed to replace the manhole cover or provide any visible warnings around the gaping hole, leaving the swirling, scalding water exposed below. A small five-year-old boy and his father were walking home from school that day when the young boy slipped and fell into the hole. Beyond reach, all the father could do was watch his son be boiled alive. After that, Robin was hesitant to ever let the kids walk ahead of her again, even to the playground.

A close personal friend of Andrei's was killed late one night while driving home after dark. Excited about his recent purchase of a new four-wheel drive Jeep, he had been out showing it off to some friends. On his way home, his headlights shown on what he thought was a rather large, but shallow, mud hole in the street. Owning a new 4x4, he thought it would be no problem to drive right through it. He unsuspectingly drove into a newly-spawned lake of scalding water large enough and deep enough to completely submerge his Jeep. He drowned in the blistering water, and city workers didn't discover his Jeep for hours. A large culvert in the infrastructure of the city's centralized hot water system had collapsed allowing the thinly paved road above to cave in, creating the lake of boiling water.

Water took the lives of many in Moscow, both hot and cold. In early 1994, Moscow recorded its lowest temperature in history, thirty degrees below zero and probably colder in the outlying areas. That night, over forty people perished from over-exposure to the cold.

All were intoxicated when they passed out in the cold, too inebriated to stand up and walk home. Perhaps like many other nights before, they thought they would just sleep it off right where they fell. But that night they never woke up.

Fire claimed lives as well. We surmised that the overstuffed trolleys, buses and trams filling the streets were merely traveling accidents waiting to happen. And it finally did. A trolley crammed with passengers during rush hour traffic caught fire, burning several people alive and severely injuring a number of others. The passengers couldn't climb out of the moving inferno fast enough.

The newspaper decided to print the story the next morning. On the front page was a picture of a woman, really a charred skeleton, laying face down in the middle of the street. She had run out into the street, while on fire, screaming blindly for help. Before anyone could get to her, she perished. Like a statue knocked off its stand, there she lay, a frozen figure memorialized in a running position for all to see. There seemed to be no sensitivity for the family and friends who knew this woman. It was newsworthy and that was that.

The Russian newspapers seemed to have few scruples when printing pictures on the front page. I was appalled to open the paper one morning and find a closeup of a woman lying face up with the top half of her head sheared off. She had been killed along with a number of other people in a train disaster. All the victims had been laid out shoulder to shoulder like victims after a battle.

The newspapers were one of only a small handful of information sources available to us, so we came to depend on them for pertinent, up-to-date news. But the daily papers also brought word of devastation.

Perhaps the most shameful article I came across was the discovery of two more of Stalin's killing fields. Tens of thousands of bodies were unearthed, revealing the cause of death: fatal gunshot wounds. One of the mass grave sites wasn't too far from us in a small Russian community just on the outskirts of Moscow. I will never forget the story surrounding it.

It seems that the KGB had informed this tiny community that they would be building a pistol range for their officers and recruits. The community watched on as the KGB constructed a tall fence surrounding the designated area. After a few weeks, the target practice began on a regular basis. Not being allowed to view any of the events due to the heavy security, the community assumed from the gunfire that it was nothing more than a target range. It was fitting that there be a fence tall enough and secure enough to prevent any stray bullets or accidents.

While the community listened on, they assumed the KGB was continuing their target practice into all hours of the night. Instead, Stalin was killing off thousands and thousands of dissidents, suspected dissidents, religious citizens and anyone accused of not being a Communist. This is where many Russians, picked up in the middle of the night and never seen again by their families, ended up. It was a terrifying reminder of totalitarianism in its most evil form.

Not all the stories we heard and read were catastrophic, ending in death. Some were really interesting and, at times, even farfetched, yet full of life and passion. Our driver and several of our Russian friends described in fairly good detail two believed-to-be historical facts that appear to be common knowledge in Moscow. I have never seen any concrete support for these, nevertheless, the Russians we met believed them with all their heart.

One story was about an "Underground City" that lay less than a block from where we lived. Along *Vernadskova* there were three towering skyscrapers that were tributes to Russia's inability to meet a deadline. Andrei informed me that they had been under construction for over ten years. As we drove by the skyscrapers each day, we noticed that the materials being used that day didn't match the materials used the day before. I don't know if they had run out of funding or supplies, but using red bricks where concrete slabs were supposed to be just didn't look right, and would most likely cause structural problems later on. Even the bricks used over a period of several weeks were different colors.

Supposedly, under those buildings and extending a mile or so westward was a massive "Underground City." We were told that it was built for the upper echelon of the Communist Party in the event of a nuclear war. Legend says the self-contained city could house the Russian Elite for up to seventy years underground if necessary.

Perhaps the lengthy construction of these skyscrapers was only a front for the Underground City's development. At face value, it would be easy to conclude that the construction above ground only received the waste left over from the construction going on below the ground.

Another story, told by many, was the legend of a monstrous tunnel connecting Moscow to St. Petersburg. The tunnel was supposedly so large that it could support an eight-lane superhighway. Russians told us that the Mayor of St. Petersburg regularly flies his small plane from St. Petersburg to Moscow and back again in this tunnel.

Sometimes the hard to believe really did happen right before our eyes.

Overnight, President Yeltsin had all the *kiosks* removed on *Novy Arbat* Street, a popular attraction for tourists, and pickpockets. In an effort to curb the rising crime wave, and to rid more undesirables, he thought it best to remove the vendor's shops, goods and all, with a large crane under the cover of darkness. The Russian entrepreneurs were outraged at coming to work and finding their business gone, building and all. Nevertheless, the Government immediately set a permit process in place and declared that if they wanted their business back, they would have to apply for the permit, but they couldn't go back to *Novy Arbat.*

In the span of one day, Customs began declaring 100 percent Duty on all items taken out of the Country.

When our building engineer, just returning from a visit out of the *CIS* [Commonwealth of Independent States], informed us of this sudden change, we all began to wonder how we would get anything out of Russia. Some, I knew, used trains to smuggle their possessions out, others used trucks, still others used friends leaving the Country by car. It was reported that those who entered Russia to buy gifts and souvenirs before the edict were seen weeping at the airport when attempting to exit after the edict, forced to either leave their treasures behind or pay the 100 percent Duty.

A day or two later, Customs retracted their 100 percent Duty charge. The turmoil came and went so quickly, only a small handful of people were subjected to the wavering and instability of the Customs Inspectorate.

In one week, President Yeltsin was able to revamp the entire Russian *ruble* system by essentially declaring chaos. He proclaimed that the entire population had less than one week to exchange their old *rubles* for new ones. It was broadcast that any *ruble* printed in 1992 or earlier, those with Lenin's face on them, was going to be worthless the following week.

It seemed to have been one more move to erase any notion of Lenin. Just as they sealed shut Lenin's tomb in Red Square -- Robin was able to view Lenin's body the day before the official closure -- the Reformers seemed intent on removing all reminders of their infamous leader.

With the sudden announcement came mad rushes to

the bank. I'm sure many Russians scrambled to pull out any money they had saved up at home. There were a number of exceptions to the announcement, for instance, the 10,000 and 50,000 *ruble* notes would still be valid and all coins would still be accepted, but many of the exceptions also changed as quickly as the declaration came.

Robin loved the new *ruble's* beautiful designs and vibrant colors compared to the American currency's drab green. Turquoise and purple being her favorite colors, the 10,000 *ruble* note with those colors made the fashion statement Robin was looking for. I believe that if she could have figured out a way, she would have preferred to wear the new *rubles* rather than spend them.

With only a couple of minor delays and setbacks, President Yeltsin accomplished his goal. He was able to capture most of the old Russian *ruble* notes, thus making any pre-1993 *rubles* collector's items. Making any *ruble*, old or new, valuable once again was a great enough feat in itself.

23
GOING
GOING
AND GONE

"It is a fair price. I will pay the money. It is not a problem," said Lydia, inspecting the list of items we had for sale. "I will take this . . . two of these . . . and all you have of that."

Tempted earlier in life to give things away to anyone with a hard luck story, I had become Russianized. I wanted to get as much money as I could for the things we were leaving behind, not that we had a lot. Besides, I had to remind myself, we had a hard luck story of our own.

Early on we had expected to extend my consulting contract for another year or two. Instead, when the contract ended, we were forced to leave Russia, partially due to Seth's inability to completely recover from a potent strain of ringworm and partially due to the increasing violence directed toward foreigners. Becoming high profile in the business community, we feared that the children would be attractive targets for mafia groups, terrorists or gypsies. Tragically, on several occasions gypsies snatched children right out of the hands of unsuspecting parents disappearing without a trace. Terrorists hijacked several school buses, demanding money or freedom. After carefully assessing everything, we felt it was time to leave, but we were returning to an unprepared and uncertain future.

When we moved into our flat, Yelena, our landlady, offered to provide everything: furniture, linens, towels, pots, pans, knives, forks and spoons. Mixing those items with the goods we lugged over from the States, the essentials were basically covered, leaving us to purchase the larger, more expensive items, such as a Russian microwave, a Russian freezer, twin-beds, as well as a VCR. These were the items Russians wanted to get their hands on. If asked, I probably would have given these things away too, or have left them in the flat as a parting gift, but it could be difficult to convince a Russian it was all right to ask for or freely accept something significant. My Russian friends had lived for so long with so little, that a good thing may have been too much. Nonetheless it brought great pleasure to offer many food, toiletry, household and Western clothing items to our friends as a small way of saying "we cared."

Not having researched our medical, food and toiletry needs very carefully, Robin purchased, and I toted, a three-year supply of razor blades, antacid, and tooth-paste to Russia, items plentiful in many of the Moscow stores. I'm confident our Russian friends are still brushing their teeth with bubblegum flavor toothpaste. Neither were the two gallons of hair spray needed, though it did make some Russian women we knew ecstatic.

It was difficult saying goodbye to such close friends. Our emotions were raw and tinged with the guilt over the culture shock compounded during the previous year. Saying goodbye to Andrei, Alla, Anton, Misha, Demitri, Valentina, Oleg, Katia, Lydia, Oxana, Lena, Julia, Svetlana, Natasha, Sasha, Sergei and the multitude of Olgas, was no small undertaking. In fact, it was one of the hardest things we've ever done, as our five-year-old son who wept hysterically and uncontrollably at one parting will attest to. We knew we would most likely never see them again.

We attended several overwhelming parties held in our honor where once again the Russians served up their very best. We were truly humbled by our comrades who elected to spend a week's salary on a wonderful dinner, serving the best Russian cuisine. It was indeed hard saying goodbye.

When Andrei pulled up, ready to drive us through Moscow one last time to the airport, we were faced once again with the unexpected. Andrei had been unsuccessful in securing his friend's large Russian van in order to transport all the luggage. All he showed up with was his little Nissan.

"I think we can do it," said Andrei, sizing up the load, and the family.

"There is no way," I said. "These bags and all of us will not fit into your tiny car."

"I think it is not a problem. Maybe we will make two or three trips to the airport."

"Andrei, we have to catch our flight before noon. Two or three trips will not be enough time to get us and our luggage there on time."

I had learned to react like a Russian when confronted with an obtrusion. I was willing to squabble just for the sake of debate. But I had failed miserably in learning to think like a Russian. Andrei was still trying to make do with very few resources and it didn't make sense. It was a mindset that may not have been that bad given other circumstances, but I reacted as a typical American suburbanite with Western expectations and an impatient attitude.

After bantering back and forth for a few minutes, an American friend, helping us load our belongings, offered the use of his Russian driver, the proud owner of a Russian van. One quick phone call and in no time, he was pulling up into the drive, ready to help out. We hastily loaded everything and then climbed in. Robin and Lindsay took off with Andrei while Seth and I rode with the driver of the van.

Getting through the airport was just as chaotic as the day we entered Russia. Some things never changed. Lugging only half the bags back through Customs we had originally brought over with us, the six large suitcases were still a handful, plus, I was now toting my bass guitar.

"Sir, where are you traveling today?" An uncommonly friendly face met us at the front entrance of the airport. Dressed in a dark blue blazer, the person was obviously a member of the airline staff.

"Helsinki and the United States," I said.

"May I see your tickets please?"

"What is this about?" I said, hesitant to hand over our only way out of Russia.

"We would like to place you on an earlier flight that is leaving in ten minutes, if you don't mind flying *Aeroflot?*"

"Why?"

"It seems that we have overbooked your original flight and we are looking for the right people who will accept our offer."

"What offer is that?"

"We will provide you and your family with a nice meal at the Helsinki Airport. Our compliments for your discomfort."

I turned to Robin who shrugged her shoulders. I nodded in consent.

In an instant, we were whisked past the long line of passengers awaiting Customs right up to the front desk.

The airline employee briefly discussed the situation with the Customs Official. After a few contentious words, the Customs Official tossed the bag he had been inspecting off the conveyer belt carrying luggage through the x-ray machine.

"Customs Papers, please?"

Our papers had stood the test of time, they were still intact. I handed them to the Official.

"How long have you been in Moscow?"

"One year exactly."

"And what did you do while you were in our city?"

"I worked as a Consultant," I said, becoming uneasy with the inquisition.

"How much money are you taking out of the country?"

"Eight-hundred American dollars," I said.

"It says you came into our country with eight-hundred American dollars, and you are leaving with eight-hundred American dollars? During your year's stay you did not find anything to purchase in our country?" he said, while intently staring at me.

Nervously, I said, "We thought it would be best to leave with what we brought with us, in order not to cause any problems."

"And the bags? You came with twenty-one and you leave with ten? Why is that?"

I noticed the people standing in line behind us beginning to grow impatient. I looked over at the Airline employee. She was pacing frantically, looking at her watch every ten or fifteen seconds.

"We had food and medical supplies that we used while we were over here. We also gave some things away as gifts." I hoped he would be satisfied with the answer.

"Let us see what is in your luggage," he said, lifting the first monstrous duffel bag up on the conveyer-belt. He flipped the switch, nothing happened. He flipped it again back and forth. He lifted the bag back off the belt and flipped the switch. It immediately started up, creaking and groaning as usual. He placed the bag back on the belt and again, it froze in its tracks.

"What do you have in here?" he said suspiciously.

"Clothes and books mostly," I said.

The flight attendant stepped in, turned her back to us and uttered a few hushed words to the Official. He looked up at us, pulled the bag off the belt and waved us through, luggage and all.

We turned to Andrei and kissed him goodbye. If I hadn't been so focused on getting out of Russia as a family unit, I might have stood there for a moment and cried with him, but before we knew it, our bags were traveling down the long conveyor belt to be loaded on the jet while we were being ushered right through the gate and into a seat.

The plane was packed, leaving little room for carry-ons. No sooner did we sit down with bags in hand than the jet began its journey backward, being pushed away from the terminal. We looked out the tiny window, trying to steal one last memory of where it all began.

In all the disorder, things seemed different then, perhaps more seasoned. It was still a typical March day, snow and ice all over the ground, but the sun was shining down upon us out of a crystal blue sky, unlike the dismal, gray day of a year before.

A flurry of memories went through my mind as we took off into Russian airspace that day. Was I frustrated? Was I sad? Did I want to leave? Was I resentful that we were, in essence, stranded in Moscow for a full year, unable to leave the city, barring our brief encounter in the country with the Russian Businessman and his associates? Was I hesitant to return to the States? Would America be different in one year's time? I didn't know. I didn't know if I wanted to know. I didn't know what I wanted.

I closed my eyes, fighting back the wave of contradicting emotions. I concentrated on the persistent whine of the jet engines and dozed off. Before I knew it, we were over the Gulf of Finland and swooping down into Helsinki.

As I sat quietly in the Helsinki airport recollecting, I attempted to mentally sum up my experience. It was difficult to choose the right thoughts to express what I was feeling. I sensed both relief and release, while at the same time I was discontented and dissatisfied with how things had ended so abruptly. The airline official had caught us completely off guard, preventing us from saying our goodbyes. I guess that is the way it was supposed to be, I thought, suddenly feeling stoic about the whole ordeal.

Living in Russia introduced me to a people who want to be just like us. They envy the privileges we have, the respect we receive, the choices we make, the freedoms we experience, and the opportunities we create. What we know as normal life, they desire to possess. They long deeply for the very same experiences most Americans take for granted every day.

I saw their desire to be like Westerners in the things they considered important to save their *rubles* for, the cars they lusted after, and the clothes they wore. Like us, they were beginning to consider materialism -- the acquisition of goods as a sign of true success -- as the answer to fulfillment in life.

Things were changing in Russia and I believe they will continue to change. I questioned many Russians, asking them if they thought Communism would ever return. Every time they unequivocally answered with a resounding, "No." They believed Russia had come too far to turn back. They may seem to be lethargic in their advancements, but Russians tend to be more methodical and deliberate than we more impulsive Westerners who have become dependent on instant gratification. They seemed determined to get there, but we may not see the fruition of their efforts in this lifetime.

Living in Russia heightened my senses to my surroundings, both physically and spiritually. The very
things the Russians have come to endure and detest as a
way of life -- the long lines, the scarcity of food, the astro-
nomical inflation rate, the unaffordable real estate, the
expensive fuel, and the eking of life -- taught me to
choose my wars very carefully. There are some things
just not worth fighting for. The elderly person, refusing
to exercise his option to turn right on red, the driver,
advancing like a snail down the highway in the left lane,
the shopper, unloading twelve items in a ten item or less
checkout stand, and the housewife, choosing to use all
the options at the ATM machine, all have their place in
this big, wide world. They have just as much right to be
here as anyone else. Russia taught me to accept these
events as part of life, and to move on. There are more
important things to expend my efforts on while I'm left
on this planet.

If my attitude ever begins to show signs of my old
ways, perhaps I'll move back to Moscow and learn for a
year again, a sentence for unrealistic expectations and
rude impatience that many Americans should be
required to serve. It would be time well spent.

EPILOGUE
ENTREPRENEUR VISIONARY AND ECONOMIC GENIUS

Millie lay motionless in her bed, staring at the ceiling, pausing only a brief moment to permit her eyes to adapt to the pre-dawn light. She was fully aware of what had startled her out of a deep sleep. She couldn't wait any longer.

Paul's come home from Moscow, she declared to herself. The thought of seeing her only son for the first time in over two years thrilled her. Envisioning Paul relaxing downstairs with his father, Ed, she quickly swung her feet out of bed, expecting to rush downstairs, throw her arms around her son's neck and welcome him home. But as her feet hit the floor, reality collided head-on with illusion. The house was dark and silent.

It was a dream, she deliberated. *No, it wasn't a dream. It was much more. It was so real. I really believed that Paul had finally come home.*

Not willing to face the cold, hard facts just yet, Millie climbed back into bed and invited the lifelike impression of her son's homecoming to stir her subconscious. The feeling it left behind was exhilarating, almost more than she could handle. Believing that there was something significant about it all, she resolved to ask Ed at breakfast if they could call Paul. Satisfied with her plan of action, she turned over, closed her eyes and went back to sleep.

Having been threatened by the Russian mafia to hand over the control of his thriving multi-million dollar business and "leave Russia or else," Paul Tatum knew that both his hotel and business center, as well as his own life, were in serious jeopardy. He believed that if he left Russia, even for a brief time, his enemies would do whatever was necessary to ensure that he would never be allowed to enter the country again, thus forcing him to forfeit any claim to the business.

In a desperate attempt to bring public attention to the impending showdown, Paul had barricaded himself in his makeshift hotel suite, turned office for the last eighteen months, while he continued to conduct business affairs via his cell phone. For his own personal safety, he hired a sizeable staff of bodyguards to protect him around the clock.

His unparalleled style of operation peaked the media's interest, which provided a platform from which he could clearly articulate threats he was receiving from the criminal underworld. But as Paul repeatedly appealed to both the US and Russian governments, Administration officials chose to surmise his claims as unfounded, unnecessary and over exaggerated. They summed him up as an ego-feeding showman who loved to bask in the limelight. Therefore, they refused to listen. In the end, they were dead wrong.

Mid-morning, Ed shuffled into the kitchen poking around for his first cup of coffee. Millie was already up and about preparing for the day. Carefully calculating when she would bring up the subject of calling Paul, she decided to begin by sharing her experience.

"Ed, I had the most vivid, lifelike impression last night," Millie said. "I awoke believing you and Paul were downstairs relaxing and 'joking about.' It seemed so tangible, I actually started to get out of bed and come downstairs to be with you. I realized then it was some sort of dream or impression I had while I slept."

"That's rare," Ed replied. "I don't recall you ever having that kind of an impression. Do you think it means anything?"

As Millie interpreted the event, she recalled the time Paul actually returned from Russia and surprised her in the middle of the night; arriving in the States on Christmas Eve. Only his sisters knew. He wanted everyone to be present for the grand entrance. Paul loved surprising people, keeping them off balance, guessing what he might do next.

After a relaxed breakfast, Millie continued where she left off, "Ed, do you think we could call him today? Just to see how he is doing?"

"Sure, I think that's a great idea," Ed said. "Why don't we call him right now."

Taken back by such an energetic response, Millie was elated. Normally, Ed was resistant to initiating the call. Not only was it expensive, but Paul was often preoccupied with business affairs. Once he was focused, he didn't want to be distracted. When Paul called home, it wasn't to discuss work. It was a time to mentally escape from the pressures of doing business in Russia. Ed didn't want to disturb him and normally preferred that they wait for him to call. But this time was different.

Ed reached for the cordless phone and dialed the number while Millie moved to the extension. The call went through the first time. It was ringing.

"Paul Tatum," came the familiar greeting.

"Hi son, this is your mom and dad. We were talking about you today and decided to give you a call," Ed said.

"Honey, I dreamed about you last night," Millie inserted.

"You did?" Paul said.

"Yes, I had the distinct impression you were here

with us," she continued.

"Sorry, my cell phone battery is about to go out. We might get disconnected here in a minute or so."

"That's okay. We just wanted to hear your voice," Millie said. "Anything going on?"

"Things are coming together. I'm about ready to win this battle legally. You're dream just might come true. I may be home for Thanksgiving."

"Wonderful," Ed and Millie said in unison. "We can't wait to see you."

"Mom, I'm in a lot better shape than the last time you saw me. I'm down to 175 pounds. I've been on a nutrient medicine with a friend and it seems to have really helped."

"Honey, that's great," Millie affirmed. "I can't wait to see you."

"My battery is about to die (they hear static in the background) so I better get off now," Paul said.

"We understand. We love you, son, and we're praying for you everyday," Ed reminded him.

"I love you too," Paul responded.

The battery died. There was silence.

I should have asked him to call us back on a regular phone. There's so much more I wanted to talk about, Millie thought. *Oh well, he'll call back in the next day or so. He always does.*

It was rejuvenating to hear Paul's voice. His positive and upbeat attitude was reassuring. They were overjoyed at the thought that he may be home for

Thanksgiving.

The next day, November 3, 1996, Paul cut short a telephone call with a friend, informing him he had been summoned to an emergency meeting with someone in the metro. He didn't say who.

He grabbed two of his bodyguards and hurried out of the *Slavayanskaya* Hotel and Business Center, making his way down the sidewalk and out the compound toward the *Kievskaya* metro, some forty yards away.

At 5:10 p.m., Paul entered the stairway leading down into the metro, totally unaware he had been set up. As he walked down the stairs, a hired assassin suddenly appeared above him, taking aim with a 5.45 caliber *Kalashnikov* machine gun. In a matter of seconds, the murderer sprayed eleven bullets into Paul's upper body. He collapsed, falling to the bottom of the stairs. The killer dropped the machine gun, already wrapped in a plastic bag, jumped into a Zhiguli, and vanished into the crowded Moscow streets. In agony, Paul whispered to one his bodyguards the name of the person whom he believed had put the contract on him. Those were his last words. By 5:20 p.m., he was dead.

Paul Tatum was the definitive entrepreneur, visionary and economic genius, a true pioneer who sacrificed his life blazing a trail of free enterprise from Washington to Moscow, often alone and against the tide . . . but that story is reserved for another book.

Square Peg Press Order Form

(Please enclose payment with your order)

Fax	(602) 813-2621
E-Mail	reunion@primenet.com

Please send the following items

Stranded in Moscow

	Price	Qty	Total
	$19.95 ea. x	_____ =	_____

About Face **Autographed Print**

	Price	Qty	Total
8x10	$25.00 ea. x	_____ =	_____
11x17	$50.00 ea. x	_____ =	_____

Sub-Total _____

Shipping $4 first book/print & $2 each book/print thereafter _____

AZ residents add 6.75% sales tax _____

Total Price _____

Amount Enclosed _____

Square Peg's Return Policy

You may return a book or print for any reason at any time.
Please contact Square Peg Press for shipping arrangements.

Your shipping address

Company Name_____

Name_____

Address_____

State_____Zip_____ Phone_____

Make checks payable to: **Square Peg Press**

Square Peg Press is not responsible for cash sent in the mail.
Sorry, no credit cards or COD's
Allow two - three weeks for delivery

For every copy of
Stranded in Moscow
sold, Square Peg Press
will make a donation to the
Paul Tatum Memorial Fund

Send mail orders/inquiries to:

Square Peg Press
PO Box 2194
Gilbert, AZ 85299